Bound for Valparaiso

The Letters of Patrick J Murray

Edited by Deirdre Roberts

First published in 2012 by
Mallaig Heritage Centre
Station Road
Mallaig
Inverness-shire
PH41 4PY

www.mallaigheritage.org.uk

ISBN 978 0 9565853 2 5

Contents

For my brother Edmund who was drowned at sea and for my Grandfather who, surprisingly, wasn't.

Acknowledgements

My thanks to those who have encouraged me to publish my grandfather's letters, especially Heather Barton. Much gratitude is due in particular to Malcolm Poole, Mallaig Heritage Centre, for his enthusiasm and his expertise in steering this particular vessel through to publication.

Valparaiso Round the Horn

Chorus:
Paddy lay back, take in your slack
Take a turn around the capstan, heave a pawl
About ship's stations, boys, be handy
We're bound for Valparaiso round the Horn

It was a cold and dreary morning in December
And all of my money being spent
What day it was I hardly can remember
When down to the shipping office I went
That day there was a great demand for sailors
From the colonies, from Frisco and from France
So I shipped upon a limey barque, The Hotspur
And got paralytic drunk on my advance

Some of the fellas had been drinking
And me myself was heavy on the booze
So I sat upon my old sea chest a-thinking
I'd just turn in and have myself a snooze
I wished I was in 'The Jolly Sailor'
Along with Irish Kate, just drinking beer
Then I thought, what happy lads were sailors
And with my flipper I wiped away a tear

Traditional

Patrick J Murray

1872 - 1956

Introduction

Laurel Place

Glasgow

16th Nov 2000

Dear Deirdre

Enjoyed your phone call on Sunday evening. Impulsive as ever, I have decided to send you the accompanying letters for your interest and safekeeping.

In 1942 during the war, when I was stationed in Wiltshire with the RAF, my father wrote to me faithfully almost weekly. When home on leave I had asked him to recount the story of his life at sea as a young man. It was the era of the great sailing ships and I had gleaned from the odd comment that he had an interesting story to tell.

His letters took the form of instalments of his life-story. Such was his enthusiasm, he became so immersed in his tale that news from home dwindled to almost nothing! I had to rely on others for that.

I am sending you also some photos from Cushendun I took this summer. When I came to the packaging of the enclosed I eventually found something suitable. I left the legend 'Do not bend' but was careful to avoid adding

'Photographs' before it. I did not want some wag in the GPO to add "Don't they?" and send them on their way duly crushed.

In haste,

Love,

Uncle Charlie

Charlie Murray

The letters which my uncle enclosed were a wonderful surprise! I found them fascinating reading and felt they were of historical significance. Towards the end of my grand-father's time at sea sailing ships were in decline and being replaced by tramp steamers. Many personal accounts of life at sea have been written by ships' officers so it is of particular interest that an ordinary young sailor recounts his tale – never having left his native glen in rural Ireland: his wide-eyed amazement when he first encountered the masts and ropes of a large sailing ship at Glasgow docks, his gaining experience of the workings and rigging of such ships, life aboard the ships, his glimpses of contemporary happenings in the wider world, his discovery of new and exotic lands.

My grandfather, Patrick Joseph Murray, was born in 1872 in Glendun, the most rugged of the beautiful Glens of Antrim. When he was seven his father died (age 50) leaving behind six children and his wife nine months pregnant. Patrick was the third oldest of these children. Four years later when Patrick was 12, his mother died and the seven children, from 4 to 16, had to fend for themselves.

Education at the village school was haphazard and school life had to fit in with the demands of the farming year. In the whole of his school career Patrick (Paddy) had a total of 141 days attendance. His teacher however, a Master Joseph Duffy, was an inspiring one who also had the foresight to teach navigation. This must have stood in good stead the many young fellows from the glen who went to sea. Such was the custom in this area of small farms with rough land and large families and lacking opportunities of alternative employment.

It was the realisation that the farm could not continue to support them all that made Paddy decide to run off to sea. He did so secretly; knowing that if he told them, his siblings would be upset and try to persuade him otherwise.

He sailed on a variety of ships from small coasters trading through the western islands of Scotland to deep-water four masted full rigged ships traversing the world's oceans. He sailed in schooners, coasters, barques, brigantines, puffers, tramp steamers and full rigged sailing ships. Along the way he encountered mutiny, gun battles, desperate situations and desperate men, storms and shipwrecks.

The letters are amazingly fluent considering Paddy's sparse schooling. The only change I have made is to introduce paragraphs and, for the sake of the narrative, create chapters. I have left his turn of phrase and occasional misspelling untouched as to alter it would be to interfere with the flow and expression of a natural storyteller.

Paddy Murray's birthplace, Cushendun

1

Leaving home

Ravenscliffe Dr.,

Glasgow.

18/11/42

My dear Charles,

Your letter reached us yesterday and found everybody quite well. Mother seems much better since we came out here. I called to see Patsy[1] today and told her you were asking for her. She is fairly well. I read your letter and noted your reminder about the promise I made to you when on my holidays. Well, I did not forget but I'm glad you reminded me for it requires a start sometime. In doing so it might be as well to let you know something of the origin of the Murray family although meantime I know but little myself beyond scraps I have been told from time to time.

Well the Murrays are the oldest family in the townland of Dunouragan, Cushendun,County Antrim. The house I was born in was built by my grandfather, Charles Murray, in 1828. At that time the family owned most of the land of

_____

1 Paddy's daughter, who lived nearby

Cushendun ca. 1903

Dunouragan and were supposed to be fairly well-to-do. My father Hugh was the eldest of the family. He was twice married. His first wife's name was Blaney who bore four children and then died. His second wife was my mother, Margaret McGee, daughter of Charles McGee of Claughey West, Glendun. There were seven of us in this second family namely Hugh, Mary Ann, myself, Neil, James, Sarah and Ellen Jane. My father was a fine judge of horses and cattle and attended all fairs. He was known as the manly little man and was too ready to go security for other men at auctions. The result was a heavy loss.

About the time I was born (1872) the family became in reduced circumstances. After my father's death our cattle were arrested for others' debts. I was then about seven years old. My mother died about four years later. We, the seven children, were to struggle with our little farm and true and loyal we stuck to each other and pulled through. My brother Hugh wished to give the farm to me so that he could go away but I would not accept. I knew that some of us would have to go some day so I made up my mind to slip off silently and that I done.

In the summer of 1890 I bought four lambs at a fair in Cushendall. In November of the same year I sold two of them to my brother Neil. The four lambs ran together on the brae until the first week in February 1891. I took the four young sheep to a fair in Cushendun and sold them, Neil's and mine, but Neil did not know until after. (I have paid him back with interest since.) Next day I was amissing.

Next instalment I'll continue the story of my wanderings.

God bless you my boy.

I remain

Your loving Father.

Ravenscliffe Drive,

 Glasgow.

24/11/42

My dear Charles,

We are all quite well here at home. My life story now continues. I think I said at the end of my last instalment that the day after I sold the four sheep I went amissing. Yes, early in the afternoon of the first Thursday of February 1891 I lifted an empty bag and took it in my hand as an excuse to go to the field for potatoes. As I turned the corner of the house I met my sister Mary who was the housekeeper and mother to the family. I said to her, "I am going to the field for potatoes". She was coming with a can of water from the spring well. After I passed her I looked back at her as she passed round the corner of the house and a great lump came into my throat. I was leaving all that I loved best in the world and besides I was the most beloved by all of them and my advice and counsel was taken in nearly everything. I knew that my brother Hugh and my sister Mary would not let me go if they knew hence my run-away.

I crossed the fields behind the neighbours' houses and got on to the Cushendall road. I looked back again then turned and footed it hastily to Cushendall and on through Waterfoot. At the end of Red Bay I went into a wee roadside shop and bought a pennyworth of cakes. Then I hurried along the Bay road until I reached a place called Fallowvee. There I waited on the mailcar returning to Larne. At last the car arrived and pulled up.

"Halloo, me bould fellow! Are you bound for Valpariso?" shouted the old driver. I jumped on and arrived in Larne, then took the train for Belfast. I got lodgings in a nice house in York Street and paid my humble bill and set out to find a fellow named Archie Walsh who left Cushendun a week before me and was staying with some friends in Belfast. I found him in a Mrs O'Mill's in Spaymount Street, smoking a new clay pipe. I waited there a few days until he was ready.

A few nights later Archie and I sailed for Glasgow in the old ship called the *Drumaderry*. Next morning we stepped of the boat at the Broomielaw, walked over Jamaica Bridge and down Clyde Place with eyes for everything except the ground! Our first destination was Mr James McSparran's, our future home when in Glasgow at 57 Clyde Place. We found it but before going in we thought we would feast our eyes on a large sailing ship moored close by at the foot of West Street.

Kingston Dock, Glasgow, 1901

We stood looking up in wonder at the great ship, her tall masts and heavy yards and a multitude of ropes and lines leading from aloft to the deck. How men could learn and remember the names of all those ropes was a puzzle to us two rustics. Little I thought then that in a few short years I would know all about them. I was then on the threshold of my young manhood. In another month I would be 19 years of age. Before we could tear ourselves from admiring the ship, we received a tap on the shoulder from another Cushendun boy, Charles O'Hara who was in one of Mrs McSparran's shops. He took us to the house where we got a friendly welcome from Mr and Mrs McSparran.

Mrs McSparran was like a mother to me and was one of my greatest friends until her death 18 months ago. May she rest in peace. She had the largest funeral that ever took place in the Co Antrim. She left behind her a family of five sons; one a priest, one a barrister, two doctors and one a farmer.

After breakfast Mr McSparran introduced us to all the boys who were staying in the house at the time. Then he took us along to one of his shops and presented us to his charge hand 'Big Rilley'. Rilley looked us up and down then said, "This young lad," pointing to me, "will soon get a berth, but in the name of God, big fellow," said he to my companion, "surely you don't intend going to sea!"

"Faith, I do!" said Archie – Walsh was about 6 feet 4 inches and walked with an awkward stoop. Three days later Mr McSparran got me a berth in a boat called the *Mandarin* as mess-room boy. I had to go to Troon to join her. It was a Saturday when I bid big Archie Walsh goodbye. We met only once since. He, poor fellow, did manage some time after to get off to sea, then drifted out of all knowledge of his

James McSparran's shop in Commerce Street, Glasgow

whereabouts. His mother and sisters looked for word from him for years but none came.

I arrived at my first ship which was bound for a place called La Rochelle, France. As the ship was not to sail until Monday morning the chief steward, Harry Downs, gave me orders on Saturday evening before he left for Glasgow to spend the weekend with his mother that I was to keep plenty of hot water in the copper boiler in the galley for the sailors to cook their food. Some time after he left I ventured a look inside the copper and found it needed a renewal of fresh water, so off I went on deck with a bucket to find the water. I met an old sailor on deck and asked him where I could get fresh water.

"Go to the burn or spring well, damn-your-skin," he replied. I asked another less gruff sailor and he showed me the fresh water pump. So I filled my copper and carried out the orders I got from the steward before he left for Glasgow. I turned in to my bunk on the Sunday night and when I awoke next morning I heard water splashing on the ship's side. I got up and went on deck. I could see nothing but water all around. The ship was at sea steaming out the Irish Channel bound for La Rochelle, France and I was on my first voyage. I was soon to know more about sea life.

The second day out we entered the Bay of Biscay, one of the worst seas in the world in stormy weather. We had very bad weather crossing the Bay. I was terribly sick. I could not look at food for three days. By the end of that time we were getting near La Rochelle and the weather became fine and fairly warm. At the same time my seasickness left me and my appetite returned with all the healthy vigour of youth. During my sickness crossing the Bay, I think I had parted with everything I had eaten during my previous life. I felt so vigorous and happy I could hardly keep from jumping up into the air. We duly arrived in port, discharged cargo and proceeded to Santander in Spain to load iron ore for Glasgow.

On our arrival at Santander the ship drew alongside the wharf and then started to load. The Spaniards put two great planks from the shore across to the hatch. These planks are about 18 inches wide and about 2 feet apart. The women start to carry in the ore in flat little baskets on their heads. The men fill the ore out of wagons into the baskets, lift it onto the heads of the women and away she goes in on one plank and returns by the other plank, dumps the ore into the ship's hold as she passes round and out for more. The women walk along as close after one another as they can. To watch them on the ship the dump of the ore from the baskets is continuous like the ticking of a clock. The ore in each basket is about 1 hundredweight. The women have a pad on the head, and so smooth and graceful can they walk that many of them can go along without a hand near the basket to steady it. These women are of all ages, some are girls, some middle-aged and some even old. I felt sorry for them although many of them sung as they toiled along. Such was the method at the time I write of (1891) but done away with long ago.

When the ship was loaded we set out for Glasgow, going out over the Bar into the open sea. We lost our propeller, were picked up by another ship and towed back into harbour where we lay for six weeks waiting for a new propeller to be sent from Glasgow. Meantime the Captain was recalled and the mate promoted to succeed him.

Next instalment in my next letter.

Dad.

P.S. My Dear Charles, you will see that there are many mistakes in both the writing and composition of my story. I can only assure you one thing, and that is, that it is you will notice that my thoughts travel faster than my pen sometimes. So cheerio until next time.

Your loving Father.

Ravenscliffe Dr

Glasgow.

My Dear Charles

The third instalment. I think I was at Santander waiting for a new propeller. The new captain just promoted took a great interest in me. He used to take me with him in the ship's boat for a sail through the harbour during our stay at Santander. On the passage to Glasgow from there he gave orders to the new mate to let me learn to steer the ship every afternoon when my own work was finished. The result was that at the end of my first voyage I could steer a ship almost as well as I ever could although I was regarded ever afterwards as a good helmsman. After our six weeks' wait for the new propeller it duly arrived and in the fitting of it I have little to record beyond that it got fitted on and we set off for Glasgow and arrived safely after a rough passage.

We loaded again for France. This time to Bayonne I think, or Bordeaux, I'm not quite sure which, and on to Bilbao, north Spain to load again for Glasgow. I have little of note to record during this second voyage except that we duly arrived back in Glasgow.

2

Schooners and brigantine

I was now getting anxious to learn to be a real sailor so I left the *Mandarin* with two regrets: namely, Captain McDonald who took such an interest in me and Harry Downs, the steward, one of the best cooks I ever met. I now have a few days with the boys from home in McSparran's who kept nobody but natives from the Glens of Antrim. In a few days I shipped in a schooner called the *Cherokee* – a small coaster which belonged to her captain. His name was Nicholson of Macramorne near Larne. The crew was composed of four. Captain Nicholson, his son, another A.B. and me - the cook. The cooking was easy. The menu was as follows: tea, bread, butter and herring for breakfast. Tea, butter, bread and herring for dinner. Tea, herring, butter and bread for supper. The vessel loaded a cargo of coal in Glasgow for Stornoway and, although it is 51 years ago [ie 1891], I remember well the passage through the Highlands.

We set sail from Glasgow, sailed out the Firth of Clyde, down along the Arran Island, round the Mull of Kintyre, up through the Sound of Jura. Anchored off Crinan for one night. Then on through the Sound of Curraghbraghan. On to

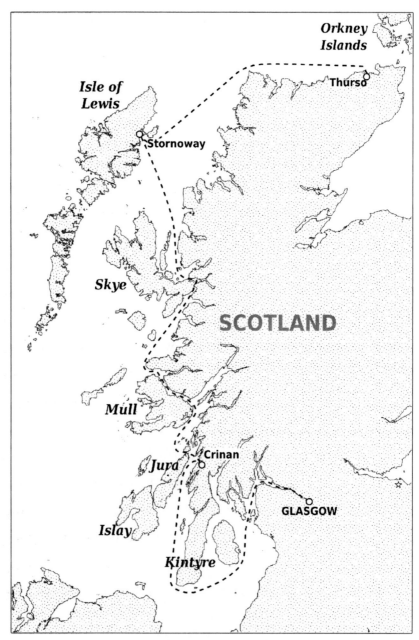

The voyage of the *Cherokee*

the entrance of the Sound of Mull to Tobermory where we anchored for a night. Next day away round into the Sound of Slate which runs north and south between the Isle of Skye and the mainland. Then through the narrows of Skye into the Sound of Rona and the Minch and eventually arrived in Stornoway. Stornoway is a fine little town, but a mile outside the town the country people and their miserable hovels of sod houses seemed a hundred years behind the times. From Stornoway we went to Thurso Bay to load slate flags for Glasgow. We returned through the same route as we went out. On our arrival in Glasgow I leave the good ship *Cherokee* feeling that I was in a good pickled condition to keep for a while after so much association with salt herring during my last voyage[1]. If you looked at a map of the Highlands you could trace the above described journey to Thurso and back.

Among the boys for a few days again and I join another schooner called the *Germina* of Arklow, County Wicklow. My last captain was Captain Nicholson of Larne. This time it is Captain Cairns of Arklow also the owner. I was cook again, but I had plenty to cook here. The *Germina* was a fine three masted vessel and plenty of good food. The crew numbered five – the captain, mate, two A.B.s and me. The Captain was a gentleman but the mate and the other two were rotters, so I leave her on our arrival in Cardiff and ship in a steamer there bound for Bordeaux, from there to Bilbao and back to Cardiff,

---

1 The *Cherokee* appears to have been lost soon after, running aground near Stranraer on 14 Dec. 1891 while carrying lime from Larne to Glasgow.

where I leave her and go to the sailors' home to lodge while looking for another sailing vessel. This last steamer was called the *True Britain*. I don't remember the name of the captain. I am about to taste of a little hardships here in Cardiff.

I am paying my way in the sailors' home as I go along. I walk round the docks two or three times a day looking for a ship without success. My money is near done. I go to the shipping office where men are signing on for voyages to all parts of the world. I have just one half crown left. A man comes up to me and says, "Hello, mate! What ship?"

"No ship," I reply.

"Come with me and I'll get you signed on a deepwater ship soon," (just the sort of ship I wished for). "Where are your clothes?"

"At the left luggage office at the station," I said.

"Come away with me and get down your bag and I'll take you to a boarding house," said he. The thought of my last half crown flashed across my mind. I went with him and got my bag out. He brought me to a boarding house in a short street off Bute Road, Cardiff. This fellow was not the householder but only a runner. The boarding master opened a door off the kitchen and showed me a little shed in the back yard and ordered me to put my bag in along with a pile of others. This boarding master was most uncivil to me. His manner made my Irish blood rise and I refused to have any food in his house. I got up and walked out and away round the dock again.

I stopped and looked at a Brigantine called the *Alfred Ray* of Portsmouth which was lying in the West Dock. I went on board, asked the captain for a berth and and to my great joy got it as an ordinary seaman to be on board for the next morning. Back I go the boarding house for my bag but the man would not let me have it unless I would pay half a month's wages although I had not one meal in his house. I went to a policeman nearby and told him. The policeman took the boarding master's part instead of mine. I slept on a seat on the vessel that night. Next morning I presented myself to the captain and told him what happened with the man of the boarding house and myself.

"Well, young fellow," said he, "You are a stranger to me and I can't advance you any money, but start work today." At night he gave me 5/- to offer the boarding house man for my bag.

I went to the house, he wasn't in. Back I came to the vessel, slept again on a seat and went back next morning at 8 o'clock to see if I could get my bag. When I arrived at the house the door was open (it was the middle of summer). I rapped. No answer. I entered the hall, asked if there was anyone in. No answer. I enter a little dining room, ask again. No answer. I looked out through the window and saw that the door of the shed where my bag was was closed with a wooden button. A sudden thought that it was not locked. I asked no more if anyone was in. No, I gently opened the door into the back, turned the wooden button of the shed door. The door flew open and the first bag I saw was my own on a pile of bags. I grasped it and away out through that hall like a racer. I could hardly believe that it could be true. Yes, I shouldered that bag and round the corner into Bute Road (one of the main streets). Just as I turned the corner I met the captain of the *Alfred Ray*. I told him how I got my bag. He nearly fell on the road laughing – he was as pleased almost as I was at the way I got the best of the scoundrel. Now you will wonder why it was that there was no-one afoot in the house. Well, I will tell you. It was the middle of hot summer weather. The man took a booze often, his wife seemed alright and easygoing. The servant girl I suppose forgot to close the door before going to bed. Anyway they seemed to be all fast asleep at half past eight o'clock in the morning. This story looks more like fiction but it's quite true.

I was happy in my new ship for I would have to learn to be a sailor, for up to now I hadn't a chance to learn. This brigantine carried a royal yard sail – that is the highest and smallest square sail aloft and, as an ordinary seaman, it was my job to loose it and to furl it. We sailed from Cardiff early in the morning for Portsmouth. I was told to go aloft and loose the royal. I climbed up and up until I got on the royal yard. I had never been up the riggin before. I was trembling, not with fear, but nervous. I loosed the gaskets of the sail and its folds fell flopping. I came down on deck and we hoisted all sail and squared away down the Bristol Channel, down south west along the Devon and Cornish coast to Land's End and round into the English Channel. Oh, what a beautiful sight! Such a sight alas I'll never see again, nor will anyone else. Why? Because there are no large sailing ships to see and very few small sailing vessels. The Channel was dotted all over with white sails. Large deep-water ships, some homeward bound, some outward to every port in the world, the scene completed by countless coasting vessels. Today I don't know of one large sailing ship under the British flag and but a few coasting schooners. Steam has swept them from the seas, I am sorry to say.

Sailing ships in the English Channel off Dover

We arrive at Portsmouth and moor at a jetty close to Nelson's famous ship the *Victory* which was used as a training ship for young navy men. The crew of our packet had to discharge our own cargo. Two of us hove up the cargo in baskets made for the purpose by a hand winch and our task was 50 tons a day. I was one of the winch men. It wasn't so hard as it sounds – we got the best of good healthy food.

Next voyage was up the North Sea to Seaham harbour. During my stay in this vessel we made several trips to Seaham and back to Portsmouth. One Sunday morning sailing in a gentle breeze through the 'Downs' off Margate, a deep-water ship was heaving up anchor outward bound on a long voyage. The sailors with handspikes were pushing round the capstan and singing a sea-shanty chorus - "Oh the fire down below!". My young heart flew out to them. I would have given the world to be with them such was my desire to get into a large sailing ship at that period of my life. At that time deep-water men looked down on steamship sailors as no sailors at all.

I finish my first year at sea next letter.

All well.

Your loving Dad.

Ravenscliffe Dr.

Glasgow.

1942

My Dear Charles

The Fourth Instalment of my life story.

I may perhaps overlap a little as I sometimes forget exactly where I left off. Anyway I was passing the Downs of Margate and proceeding towards the Solent Firth, the approaches to Portsmouth Harbour. We made several trips between Portsmouth and Seaham. By this time I was getting quite good at climbing and confident. One day while working discharging in Portsmouth the mate let go the whip, or rope, which we used to heave up the tubs of coal out of the hold to a platform where the coal was weighed. The whip ran up to the gin or pulley at the derrick head and the hook on the end of the whip got stuck in the gin. The mate and the others just looked up and for the moment seemed not to know what was the best way to get it down. I, without being told, slipped up the riggin, onto the masthead, onto the lift or rope that held the derrick head up. I slid down to the derrick head, got astride, reached down to the lead-block, got hold of the hook and overhauled it down to the deck again in a moment. Everybody watched me in surprise. A stranger passing asked, "Where does that lad come from?". This surprise gave me the impression that they had never seen such a thing done before. I just tell you this little incident to let you see that I soon got over the nervous feeling I experienced the first time I was sent aloft leaving Cardiff. Now, you will think it strange that I do not remember the name of the captain or any one of the crew of this vessel – the *Alfred Ray* – while I have a clear recollection of the vessel. It is just 51 years ago since then.

It is now the end of summer. The *Alfred Ray* goes this time to Cardiff. When we arrive there I get homesick so I leave her and make my way to Glasgow where I prepare to go home for Christmas. In due time I arrive home in Cushendun quite a proud lad with a sailor bag on my shoulder. Sailors were well thought of in the district. Cushendun, Cushendall and Red Bay produced many seamen and some of the most brilliant captains of their day. To name but a few – there were Captain McDonnell of Glenariff, who was captain of the famous clipper *Donald McKay,* [which] broke the record to and from Australia. His age at the time was 29. Captain McCambridge from Glendun, Captain Hamilton of Cushendun, Captains Blaney, Delargy and McDonnell from Cushendall and others too numerous to mention here. All are delighted to see me – the wandering boy home again. I stay at home for about 5 or 6 weeks then get ready for away again. I nearly always felt deeply sorry leaving home and was some distance on my way before my sorrow wore away.

3

Shipwreck and mutiny

I arrive in Glasgow on my second year (1892). After some days wait I get a ship. This time it is a schooner called the *Lively Lass*. Captain Dan McCart of Waterfoot, Glenariff, a cousin of James McCart, your mother's uncle, was the captain. The mate was Charles O'Neill – father of four sailor sons. I am the ordinary seaman. I stay for most of the summer in this vessel trading to the west of Ireland. Captain McCart was also owner as well as captain. He was a very clever captain, cautious and capable. He fed us fairly well during the day but allowed us nothing during the watches of the night. I left her in the month of June of that year and joined another schooner called the *Exit* of Campbeltown.

The captain of this vessel had only one arm. He got the other blown off by a rocket in a previous shipwreck. He was also captain and owner. This vessel loaded a cargo of coal for a jetty near Bonawe in Loch Etive. All went well until we dropped anchor in a little bay at Connel Ferry – the entrance to Loch Etive. This place Connel Ferry is a dangerous place for strangers. It is the narrow bottle-neck through which all the water at flood and ebb must pass that fills and empties

Connel Ferry, ca. 1895

**The shipwreck of the *Exit*
reported in the *Oban Times***

CONNEL FERRY.

SHIPWRECK IN LOCH ETIVE. — The *Exit*, of Campbeltown, from Glasgow to Ardchattan with coal, on Tuesday last, when attempting the passage of the rapids of Lora, struck on the reef of rocks on the north side of the channel and stuck fast there. As she was heavily laden, and the tide running very strong, the crew took to the boats, at the same time removing their clothes. The vessel was thrown on her beam ends, broadside on to the tide, and little hope was entertained of getting her afloat again. The crew, however, stood by her in their boat, and at the end of two hours she floated off, and in doing so a large piece of her keel was wrenched off. The crew immediately boarded her and endeavoured to run her ashore, and after being hauled up to what is called Little Connel, they got a rope ashore and had the fore-part of the ship aground, when she heeled over and sank in deep water, and must have gone on her side, as she totally disappeared for some hours. The crew, supposing she was floating under the water, made a close search over Ardchattan Bay, but the main mast again appeared above the water at the place where she went down. It is feared she will be a total wreck. Much sympathy is felt for the Captain, who is the owner, as it is understood here that the vessel is not insured.

the large expanse of the whole loch; besides, right in the centre of this narrow entrance there is a rock awash at low water, submerged at high water. The tide turns so quickly in a moment it's like a busted dam either way.

At the turn of the tide we hove anchor and set sail for the gap between the rock and the mainland but the tide soon carried us right onto the rock. Fortunately we had the small boat towing behind as she struck. The small boat swung round to the shelter of the leeside. The vessel, whilst heavily listed, still hung on the rock while we sprackled into the small boat with anything we could grab of our belongings. Soon willing help came from the shore. Several small boats shoved off to us. The men from the shore took our bags and left them safe ashore. Then we, with a number of other boats, dogged to leeward of the ship which we were afraid might turn-turtle at any moment. Thus we stayed until near high water when the vessel slipped off the rock and up-righted.

We, with several other boat crews climbed aboard but, alas, too late. The water was beginning to cover the deck. She was slowly sinking. As she drifted with the tide close to the west shore where there were plenty trees growing, we ran a long line ashore, tied it to a tree and hauled her in close in order to beach her. The Captain wished to stay on and go down with his ship but we just grabbed him and pushed him into the boat. No sooner than we done so than down she plunged stern first. We were only just clear of her. Not only did she sink but went clean out of sight – masts, yards and sails which were still set. I saw her stern blow out with coal gas as she disappeared.

We stood on the beach gazing at the spot where she sank, the old captain a pathetic figure in our midst and no wonder, for all he had in the world had gone to the bottom. About a quarter of a mile down the loch, where the water spreads out, her masts and yards came up, the tops still hanging, but the hull never appeared. She had drifted onto a sandbank.

We were taken that night to a little farm house on the Fort William side of the Loch where the old man and wife gave some of us their own bed to sleep. They were most kind to us. Next morning the masts peeped up the same. A carpenter living in the district offered the captain £10 for the vessel as she lay on the bank. The captain took it and paid us our wages. I never felt so sorry to take money from anyone as I did on that occasion. I was only 10 days in the ship. There were five of a crew all told. After receiving our wages we got rowed over to the Connel ferry side, got the Oban train to Glasgow. So I never heard of the old captain ever after.

I don't remember a single name of one of the crew but I remember the young cook was a Highland lad, the mate was a Ballywalter man – Co. Down, on Strangford Lough near where Mr Ferie's craft was wrecked, the A.B., I forget where he belonged, I was an Ordinary Seaman. Long after I made enquiries about the vessel. The carpenter who bought her thought he might be able to raise her by means of empty barrels tightened around her at low water but he failed to do so, and so she lay for years. If ever you come across anyone living at Connel ferry or on the opposite shore, especially the old folk, you could, I think verify this story. I'll tell you who might be able to find out some information in connection with it – Miss Fraser of St Joseph's who is teaching not far from the scene of which I write (the year 1893).

I was only a few days in Glasgow when I was invited to join a little coaster steamer called the *Loch Gair* trading often up through the Highlands. We went several times to Loch Etive and once to Portree, Isle of Skye; sometimes to Belfast. The captain was William O'Kane of Glenarm who is still living. I was speaking to him the last time I was in Ireland. During my short time in this little steamer I used to slip up on deck and have a try at driving the steam winch while the captain and the others were below having their meals in harbour. By such means I gained a little knowledge of driving a winch. The only incident of any note which is worth a mention in the *Loch Gair* is that one foggy night while making for the locks on the Crinan Canal we ran hard on the rocks in front of the Crinan Hotel but managed to back off at high water.

Christmas comes and I go again to see the old home and enjoy the love of sisters and brothers and the friendship of our neighbours. My stay at home lasted about four or five weeks. Then I prepare for the road again. The parting from those one loves always causes a feeling of sorrow. Such was mine nearly always as I left the old homestead.

Glasgow is my starting point. I join the *Loch Gair* once more. I stay in her a short time then leave her in the month of June. I am anxious to get away deep-water as going in large sailing ships was termed. I had not long to wait. My good friend Mrs McSparran got me a berth as ordinary seaman with her cousin Captain Dan McDonnell in a large four-masted full rigged ship called the *Norma*. She was the first steel sailing ship that hailed from Cardiff. She was built in the Barclay, Curles & Co yard on the Clyde. This ship was brand new, going on her maiden voyage.

At the end of June she towed from Glasgow to Newport to load 4000 tons of coal for Rio de Janeiro, Brazil. This ship when she sailed from Cardiff had on board almost a whole Irish crew. Robert Duff of Islandmagee – a tyrant, but a thorough seaman, was the mate. A.B.s were Dan Carlin from Derry, two from Dublin, two from Limerick, two from Arklow, one from Wexford, one from County Down and a couple of Swedes. There were four ordinary seamen – one from Glasgow, Sonny Blaney, and three from County Antrim – John McSparran Carnlough, Johnny McDonnell Cushendall and myself from Cushendun. I nearly forgot James McAuley A.B., also from Cushendun. The cook and steward – I don't remember where they came from - and one from Glasgow. This *Norma* story is a long one. I'll continue it next time.

Dad

❋

Ravenscliffe Dr.

Glasgow

My Dear Charles,

Continued the voyage of the *Norma*.

The *Norma* sets sail for Rio. We leave Newport in tow, for a distance down the Bristol Channel, while the sails are being loosed and got ready for setting. All being ready the sails are hoisted and the ship heads out past Lundy Island into the open sea. The wind is blowing fresh from the west. We have to tack for days. When the ship gets well out to the west, we sheer off to the sou-west and get a long slant that carries us along past the Azores where we catch the south-east trade winds. The weather is now steady and warm. These trade winds usually last for many weeks and take you right into the Doldrums near the Line. The Doldrums are a series of calms which may last for days, perhaps weeks. Crossing the Line (the Equator) is an event in the life of a sailor. If it be his first time he must get shaved, the razor is a wooden one and the soap is usually a mixture of tar and other ingredients. After the shave he is thrown into a tarpaulin filled with water. If he kicks against his treatment he is roughly handled. In the case of the *Norma* those of us who had not crossed the line were in the majority. So, fearing a mutiny, the captain gave a bottle of whisky to each side for peace. The old hands readily accepted the terms so I crossed the Line without a shave.

On the passage out from Cardiff to Rio de Janeiro I was the only one of the Ordinary Seamen who could take the wheel, and did take my turn with the Able Seamen. It so happened that it was my wheel going into Rio past the famous sugar-loaf – a high peaked mountain on the port side of the entrance to the great harbour of Rio de Janeiro. This great harbour was a sight to see at that time. Miles of great sailing ships at anchor discharging into barges. It was a beautiful sight with their lofty masts and yards like a great plantation with the leaves blown away. Alas a sight I, or anyone else, will never see again. The *Norma* takes her place among them and drops anchor.

The Brazilian Navy shelling Rio de Janeiro, 1893

Here we landed in the heat, not only of the sun, but in the middle of a revolution - the Brazilian Army against the Navy. The President refuses to demit office and the Army supports him. The Admiral of the Fleet demands his resignation, the navy is with him. The navy tries to land. The army sees that they don't. Every street or opening to the sea front of the city is guarded by soldiers. Any boat seen mooring at night, or approaching the shore, is promptly fired on by the soldiers.

The next day after our arrival the barges came alongside and the discharging began. There is a 'donkey-boiler' on the ship for hoisting the cargo from the hold. Seven men and myself are sent into the main hold to fill the coal into baskets. Each man fills his own basket. I have to fill mine with the A.B.s, the other three Ordinary Seamen get lighter jobs. McSparran is put to look after the 'Donkey', Blaney to clean brass and clean about the deck, John McDonnell is put on night watchman. The A.B.s. thought I wasn't getting a fair deal from the mate. We worked hard under the burning sun, besides the food was very bad. The mate was a narker. The men are beginning to grumble under his tyranny. The third day he began to rush us still more. He bawled down at us to put a spurt on. When he went away from the hatch, one of the Limerick men said that if he came back with any more rushing we would down tools.

"Well," said Dan Carlin (the Derryman) who was my hero, "I joined this ship to make the round voyage in her but, if you are all agreed, I am with you."

Shortly afterwards back comes the mate to the hatch, yells down at us again – first at me, then at all of us. No sooner did he do so than we down shovels and up the ladder on to the deck. My fellow seaman from Cushendun, James McAuley, was the last man up. I stood near the hatch for fear he would 'funk', a fear that was confirmed the next day. The mate was taken aback by this sudden act. He asked us where we were going, but we answered him not. The captain, who was ashore in his boat at the time, came aboard shortly after. He called us all aft and wished to know our grievance. Dan Carlin was our spokesman.

Carlin replied, "We'll tell the British Council our grievance when we get ashore."

"Alright," said the skipper, "I'll have you all in jail in an hour."

"Thank you," said Carlin. Meantime we were ordered back to the forecastle.

The captain went ashore to report us to the British Council, but it so happened that the Council had cleared from his office because a building close by had been blown down by a shell from a man-o-war lying in the bay. A duel between the Army and the Navy was now a daily occurrence.[1] Back aboard came the captain. This time he was in a different mood. He called us all aft again and appealed to us to turn to and he would forgive us for our offences. We refused his

---

1 Other sources record that the crew of the *Norma* constantly had to take refuge from flying bullets when discharging and that a ballast lighterman was killed by a rifle bullet.

offer. Then the mate got other men to take our clothes from our quarters to the cabin and locked them up there. We were confined to one side of the forecastle. Through that night the mate kept dodging about trying to induce us to turn to again.

Next morning four of our eight rebels surrendered, among them James McAuley, thus reducing our number to four – namely: Dan Carlin, the Limerick fellow (I now forget his name), Jim Weldon (a Co. Dublin man) and myself. Us four die-hards were then separated from the rest of the crew and put on bread and water. For three days and nights we were kept like this. On the third night we held council of war and decided to escape by means of the captain's boat which was hauled up to the davits but not swung in board at night. Now the problem was, how could we manage to get the boat away, it being hung up just beside the captain and officers' quarters, besides a night watchman on night duty parading the deck. Another danger was the mate was supposed to have his revolver ready in case of our attempted escape.

However at three in the morning we set out along the deck. We confronted the watchman (Johnny McDonnell, a young fellow I liked). The dauntless Dan Carlin spoke to him and said, "McDonnell, we are taking the captain's boat and you keep quiet."

"For Heaven's sake don't take the boat or I'll be killed!" Poor chap, he was afraid of the mate.

"We are taking the boat and if you make a sound, over the side you go!"

"Well do something with me," said the lad in terror. I took him to the main fife rail at the base of the main mast, tied his hands behind his back to the pin rail, put a big scarf round his mouth but left his nose free to breathe. Having thus secured him (to leave him blameless) we stole along to the boat. Carlin jumped into one end of the boat, 'Limerick' into the other end, Jim Weldon and I stayed on deck to get the tackle falls all clear, then passed the falls into the boat so that we could lower ourselves, then Jim and I hopped in. Then down she goes with a rattle. The bow end ran quicker than the stern end and she nose dived a bit into the water but uprighted. In ten seconds we had unshackled and were pulling away with all our might. I was on the bow end.

The night was calm. We could hear the hubbub aboard. We expected a longboat to follow us. If they had we were prepared to fight but they didn't follow. We heard afterwards that Mick O'Brien, the second mate (a brother-in-law of the captain's) tried to get a boat's crew to follow us, but they refused. Now, we had to pull away in the opposite direction from the city or we would have been shot by the soldiers who kept guard round the seafront of the city in order to keep any of the Navy from landing. This great harbour spread out for many miles.

As day was breaking we pulled into a little bay and on the beach stood a number of fishermen who refused to let us land. Dan Carlin to the rescue. He could speak some of their language and offered to make them a present of the Captain's boat. It took a trick. They let us land and took their prize. The boat was worth at least £50 at that time – about a couple of hundred now. We, the four of us, stood on the sand looking at one another. Carlin drew from his pocket a two-shilling piece and reached it to me saying, "Murray, you are the best lad I ever met. Take this - it's all I have." I did not want to take it but he made me take it. This 2/- was the only worldly goods possessed by us four rebels.

4

Rio de Janeiro

We then set out to walk to the city seven miles distant. We were favoured by not having anything to carry because our belongings were locked up aboard ship. We arrived there and got us into a hard-up boarding house kept by a man called Mack Russell, a Liverpool man, married to a Portuguese woman. The landlord was a scoundrel who made his living by picking up sailors in distress and 'shanghaiing' them in some ship, drugging them, putting them aboard and receiving a month's wages for the job! These ships were mostly bound for fever pots and could not get crews in the ordinary way. There were several other fellows staying at the same place. We got two meals a day, fed in a yard like cattle. Our menu consisted of black beans, a small roll and a cup of coffee for breakfast. The same in the evening. Half a mile away we slept in an old loft on straw beds on the floor. No blankets or covering. We were like this for a week. Suddenly Russell went amissing. For two days no word of him. His wife told us if he didn't turn up next day she could not keep us any longer. Next day came and no tidings of Mack Russell. We got our last meal.

Although Dan Carlin was my 'hero', Jim Weldon was my chum and by reason of the fact he was a teetotaller like myself. Whereas Carlin, 'Limerick' and the others could enjoy and did – when they could get it – a 'stone of paratee' (a glass of brandy). It was cheap – a penny a glass. A man could get drunk for about fourpence. After breakfast, Jim Weldon and I walked down the street down-hearted and forlorn not knowing how or where we would get our next meal for my 2/- was spent. The only place we could hope for was a convent on the outskirts of the town. This fellow Weldon was a very modest and shy young man, although a bit older than I was. As we were passing the end of the street were we slept at night, I happened to look across the street. As I done so I saw a well-dressed man looking over at us. As I looked he put up his finger and motioned me over to him. Over both of us goes.

"Well," he said to me, "do you want a job, young man?" I need hardly tell you I was only too willing to say yes. "And do you?" said he to Weldon.

"Yes," said Jim.

"Could you get me a few other men to go on board to work cargo?" We said we thought we could – thinking of Carlin and Limerick. This man was the chief officer of an Aberdeen boat trading on the coast out there. He then told us where his ship was lying. So off we went to hunt up Carlin and Limerick. After a search we found them, but they wouldn't go.

The mate was already there when we arrived and told him our search for other men failed. "Alright," said he, "Turn to!" He brought us aboard to work cargo. She was loaded with silver sand and pit props. When we got on board he looked at me and asked where I belonged to.

"Belfast," I replied (thinking he would not know where Cushendun was and as Belfast being the nearest port to my native place).

"I'm a Belfast man myself," said he. "Could you drive a winch?" he asked me.

"I can a little but I'm not very capable," I told him, which was just the naked truth for I had only the meagre experience that I had learned in the little steamer *Loch Gair*.

"Well, try your hand," said he, "and I'll send the nigger down below to work cargo". The negro was the man at the winch. The officer thought the winch would be a lighter job for me. This mate was like a father to me. I started at the winch and concentrated all my attention on my work. I never made a mistake. I repaid his trust and kindness. The man who engaged us was the Chief Officer of the boat which was trading on the Brazilian coast. Taking his cargo of silver sand to Rio and transhipping it into British and German liners calling there on their way round the Horn. Our little ship would pull alongside these large liners and discharge a consignment into them. Then draw off and wait on the next liner that would call. Thus we were two weeks discharging the boat.

We were paid four milreas a day, roughly 5/- and food and plenty of it. At the end of our fortnight we had 40 milreas or about £2/10/0 saved. He also asked us to sleep on board at night so interested was he in our welfare. This kind man asked us to join his little ship on the coast there. Jim and I agreed to do so when all of a sudden he and the captain had a dispute so this good friend left, and so did we. Jim Weldon and I came ashore out of that ship with about three pounds in English money each. We never met the mate again but to me he was a real friend and like a father to us.

Your loving Dad

*

Ravenscliffe Dr

Glasgow

My Dear Charles

By this time, and before we left the coaster, our esteemed boarding master Mack Russell had turned up and found out where we were working. He had pickets put on watch for us and made an open boast that he would shanghai the two of us. Now having money we did not go back to Russell's. Weldon and I made our way to the sailors' Bethel, it being the only place a British subject was safe. We had money now so could pay for a cot-bed for a milrea at night. During the daytime we had a cup of coffee and a roll at a kiosk on the

The Port of Rio, 1900

street whenever we felt like it. Such was our routine for about a week after leaving the coaster.

Meantime we knocked about the streets. We saw some exciting happenings. One morning Weldon and I went out on a little hill on the west side of the city to have a look at our old ship *Norma*. We could see the men walking about the deck. While thus standing watching out at the ship, suddenly a man-o-war came racing into sight and opened fire sending shells up over the city. The few stragglers who were on this open space ran for shelter. When we reached the street there was a panic. Women were running out of their houses with children in their arms. Weldon and I made our way to the sailors Bethel which was flying the British flag.

We heard a Glasgow ship called the *Kinrosshire* was to sign on some hands and a man named Mr Murphy had the contract of finding the men for her. I saw Murphy going round a corner on the day the ship was to sign. I went up to him and asked the job for Jim and I.

"If you are in a boarding house I can't have anything to do with you," he said.

"We're not in a boarding house," said I. "We are staying in the sailors' Bethel".

"Oh! You are just the sort of men I am looking for," said he. He then told us where to go at 11 o'clock that morning and he would take us to the British Council's office to sign on. So Jim and I arrived on the spot to time. Meanwhile another captain had gone to Mr Murphy asking for two men. So instead of the *Kinrosshire* it was a ship called the *Mylomene* of Liverpool we signed on. On such occasions one has to give the name of his last ship. I gave the name of an American schooner I never heard of and Weldon done similar. Just a matter of form, the Council just winks at such things. Anyhow we were signed and I a full fledged Able Seaman. The captain told us where his boat would be waiting to take us off to the ship. Meantime Mack Russell had four pickets at different points watching in case we would slip him but the two greenhorns did slip him and eluded his touts and arrived safely on board the full rigged ship *Mylomene* bound for Port Adelaide, South Australia.

Now before leaving Rio, I must record an exciting incident. I have previously told you of us being warned by Mack Russell's wife that if her husband did not turn up she could not keep us any longer, and of us receiving our last meal of black beans and coffee. On the night before, in the old house where we slept on the floor of a loft, which was about half a mile distant from the boarding house, a number of soldiers were stationed at the foot of the street which opened onto the waterport. During the day some of our fellow lodgers had picked up a fellow who got paid off a ship and so had some money. They had been drinking together and had brought the sailor into our sleeping quarters for the night. In the middle of the night they quarrelled and started a fight. Jim Weldon and I done our best to peacify them but in vain. We who were sober knew the danger for at the end of this street there were a batch of soldiers day and night to keep watch on the Navy, and these soldiers were anything but friendly towards Britishers.

We managed to quiet them down for a while, but not for long. The row started up again. This time Jim Weldon got hold of the strange sailor – 'Scotty' we called him – to put him out for peace. As Jim was leading him by the arm to the stair a big fellow named Eritty who was the cause of the row lifted a piece of a broken shovel to cleave 'Scotty' on the back of the head. As he raised the shovel to strike, I jumped and pulled it out of his grasp. 'Scotty' never knew how near he was to that vicious blow. As Jim Weldon and his charge reached the foot of the stair, the door burst in and two shots were fired.

"Great God!" I said to myself "that's poor Scotty gone!" As I stood there, at the head of the dark stair, in very great fear, I prayed an earnest prayer to the mother of God to save us. I most certainly thought it was our last night in the land of the living for the soldiers could just do as they pleased with civilians. After the shots were fired everything was dead silent for a while. I wondered what had become of my chum Jim. I went down the stair to look for him. As I crept to the door in the black darkness I put out my hand to feel my way. I found him standing in the doorway.

"What are you doing standing here?" I said to him. He did not speak but caught my arm and pressed it as a warning to keep quiet. As I stepped on to the flagstone at the door beside him I found the muzzle of a rifle pressed against my breast. I said instinctively, "Sparem poka" – the only words I knew of their lingo. It meant 'wait you a little'. The nigger pulled down the gun and stood at guard of the door. In a moment when I recovered my calm, I tried to make the soldier understand that the cause of the noise was drinking Parratee (brandy). He could not speak English but he understood what I was trying to explain to him by his nod. Thus we were, Jim and I, could not go in or out.

After a long time soldiers came rushing up the street. About 20 yards from the door they were halted. The negro soldier guarding the door spoke a whole litany to the officer in charge, I'm sure explaining our position. After he finished the officer spoke in bad broken English, and he did not bother to use the mildest of the English language. Oh no! He called us all the Englosterra beachcombing bastards he could try tongue to. He ordered us inside and to keep quiet or he would shoot us. Well, we all obeyed that order very promptly and thankfully. Thanks to the holy Mother of God. I prayed that night that if I was spared through till morning I would never sleep or try to sleep in that den again. It was the next morning Jim Weldon and I met our good friend the mate of the Aberdeen coaster so we were saved from want and hunger ever after.

During our four weeks in Rio we saw some harassing sights. I saw the bombardment of the Fort by the Navy, but the Fort held out. I saw the streets in holes and mules and tackles falling into the holes. I saw a crowd of Liverpool beachcombers prowling about the streets who would cut your throat for half a dollar. Among these beachcombers was a gall fellow known as 'Belfast'. He hailed from that city. This Belfast boy was a desperate but brave fellow. His favourite pastime was tackling wild men. Unless you had the name of being a fighting man you were quite safe but if a fellow had the reputation of a fighting man Belfast would go and test his pluck right away. One morning a lot of us was squatting at a place called Parliament Square when a sailor the name of Donnelly who got paid off a ship, and who had the name of being a terror, passed by.

"That's Donnelly, the fighting man," said one of the fellows.

"Who?" said Belfast.

"There crossing the street," someone shouted. Up jumps Belfast and after Donnelly he goes. Stops Donnelly right in the middle of the street.

"Are you a fighting man?" asked Belfast. What the reply was we did not hear, but in ten seconds they were at one another like two dogs. Donnelly went down three times in quick succession. In five minutes the fight was over and Donnelly the bully was down and out.

As I have now recorded, I think, most of the Rio incidents except one. During the week between our leaving the little coaster and our signing on the *Mylomene* Dan Carling and Limerick, Big Eritty, Jim Weldon and another decided to set off to walk to Santos. There there were supposed to be ships lying without a crew, who having died from a fever, wages were rumoured to be £10 per month. Jim Weldon consented to go. I refused to leave Rio and face a journey of 300 miles over mountains. I begged Jim Weldon not to go, but in vain. So I conveyed my chum about a mile outside the city, bade Weldon and Carlin goodbye with a heavy heart. I returned to the sailors' Bethel, sat down at a table looking into space, feeling sad and lonely. I don't know how long I sat there, but about an hour later, to my great joy, Jim Weldon arrived back with the assurance that he would never leave me again. I heard later that my 'hero' Dan Carlin died on the journey. I could never find out if the report was true or not. I only know that I was sorry for him, for I loved the brave fellow.

The hardships, thrills and dangers of Rio shall not fade from my memory. Now I think I'll lift anchor and leave Rio de Janeiro.

Dad

PS I hope I'm not boring you with these incidents.

5

Rio to Australia

Ravenscliffe Dr.

Glasgow

My Dear Charles

We sailed out past the Sugar Loaf on Friday the 13th of October 1893 on the full rigged ship *Mylomene* bound for Port Adelaide, South Australia – a day and date I am not likely to forget. A cockney sailor on board said as we passed out the head, "Go–blamy! Sailing on Friday and 13th as well – unlucky day to sail!" I never heard the remark before. But anyhow, every weekend until we reached the Australian coast we had gale after gale of wind.

We had a terrible passage running the Eastern down to Australia. One Saturday evening it started to blow a hurricane. Through that night we lost most of our canvas. We began late in the evening to shorten sail. As the sheets were slackened to clew up they blew into ribbons. Twice that night I was nearly thrown off the yardarm into the sea. During the night, the main sail which was furled – what was left of it – pockets of wind were getting into the loops and blowing it out of the gaskets. The mate came and asked the men to go aloft and try and secure it before it blew away. The men filed out on deck and made for the main riggin. An old sailor named Cowan, of Bath, took the lead up the riggin. I was at his heels. He was first out along the yardarm. The ship was bucking heavily. I got alongside Cowan on the yard footrope. I looked round for the others who never left the deck, not only so, but had returned to the shelter of the forecastle.

The *Mylomene*

I turned to Cowan and said, "The others have turned tail".

"Well," said he, "we can't do anything without more help." Neither could we. Just at that moment the ship gave a very heavy lurch and carried away the lee mainyard lift – that is the rope or stay that keeps the yard level, so the yard went swaying up and down. How we held on I can't tell. All I know is that a loose rope swung past me. I got hold of it and slid down on to the deck about the quickest I ever done. That finished us for that night.

Next morning (Sunday) the gale was spent. It fell calm which was worse than half a gale. The sea was rolling mountains high and no sail to steady the ship. We had to start and pull up another suite of canvas from the sail locker and bend it on which was no small job. All day on Sunday we laboured bending on new canvas. The third officer said it was a night to be remembered and so it was.

Afterwards we had a fine passage down to Adelaide. No incident happened except that I had a fight with a big Russian–Finn and he gave me the sorest beating I ever got. He was a great big sturdy fellow and much older than me. I thought because I was a Britisher and he a foreigner I could beat him but no, he could hit out like the kick of a horse. I was sore for weeks after but I let no-one know. We fell out about a mere nail in the side of a bunk. What a trifling thing to fight about, but such is the folly of youth.

We arrive safely at Port Adelaide and wait for orders which we soon get, to proceed to Sydney and to load wool and tallow for London. Sydney is the most beautiful harbour in the world. It is dotted with little isles and the city has a great park. The people are most friendly. Fruit and food are plentiful and cheap. Our ship entered Sydney harbour on New Year's Day 1894.

The *Mylomene* lay at circular quay in Sydney for six weeks loading. No great incident of note occurred during our stay there except a fight on deck by a couple of the crew and just when it was proceeding on a Sunday afternoon a fellow named Barney Black from Glenariff came on board to see me from another ship. He, Barney, was a good joke. He had one squint eye. Coming off the gangway he looked aloft and said, "She's a fine ship." Then he turned his gaze on the two fellows fighting and said, "and a damn hard case into the bargain."

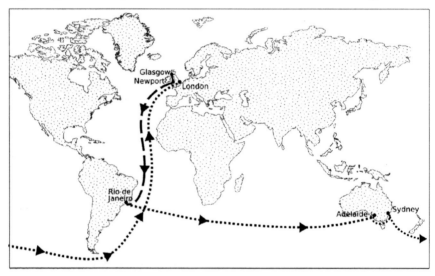

The voyages of the *Norma* and the *Mylomene*

We sail from Sydney for London away round Southern Island of New Zealand and squared away to run the Eastern down for Cape Horn. We experienced the expected gales on this run to the Horn. In a gale running before the wind two men are called to the wheel. On the night we were to round the Horn I was called out to stand by the man who went before me in turn. The man who stands by the lee wheel during his two hours. Now this old salt who I followed was a jealous old rap and to take me down a peg he said to me some minutes before four bells, "You'll not have to take a wheel with a night like this." The way it was said nettled me, as if I would not be trusted with the wheel that night. I said nothing, but thought hard. I soon made up my mind. When the bell struck 4 I stepped up to the weather side and took hold of the wheel which was my place. He gave me the course then stood for a moment looking at me.

"Are you taking the wheel yourself?"

"I am," said I. At this moment my feet were frozen but I determined to stick it and stick it I did. And no-one called to stand by the lee wheel for me.

About 7 bells the mate who was on watch came to me. "Murray," said he, "you shouldn't have taken the wheel. The next two men should have relieved you at 4 bells." Well, I just told him why I stayed the four hours at the wheel and what old Fleming said to me.

"I would not let a man aboard the ship say that to you. I'll back you against the best man aboard. Why," said he, "the deck is almost dry." A great compliment for steering before a gale, for if a ship is swerving from side to side the deck won't be long dry. So I had my own back on the jealous old Fleming although I suffered some cold feet. We rounded the Horn that night and changed course north up the South Atlantic for the Line and tropical weather and finally arrived in London safely – a full fledged Able Seaman – in June.

Dad

Ravenscliffe Dr.

Glasgow

My Dear Charles

Jim Weldon and I get paid off the ship *Mylomene* in London and take the train for Cardiff. After a week or two there we ship in a steamer called the *Ruperra* loading coal for a place called Selonica in the Black Sea. We discharged there and loaded maize for Cork in Ireland. From there back to Cardiff where there was a sailors' strike on. We leave the *Ruperra* and join the strikers, Havelock Wilson at our head. The strike turned out a failure so Jim Weldon and I had to separate and go in different ships.

I joined a coasting schooner called the *J. B. Wood* bound for Galway, west of Ireland. The captain James Pollard was a Cornishman and a spiritualist in religion. After leaving Cardiff he (the Captain) came along the deck to me and said, "You are an Irishman?"

"Yes," I replied.

"I suppose you have heard of the man called St Patrick," said he.

"I have," said I.

"Well," said he, "if he was living now the people would kick him."

"Oh, would they?" I returned. He then proceeded to say a ridiculous thing about a priest in the west of Ireland. I just wheeled around and called him a damned liar and challenged him to prove it whereupon he never again spoke a word to offend me. Not only so, but promoted me in a few months to be mate of his vessel. On another occasion when we were in a little port called Shoreham in Sussex we lay at a jetty on the opposite side of the river from the town. I tried to push a boat which lay on the river bank into the water to go to Mass on a Sunday morning. I found the job a difficult one but this same captain came to my assistance without me asking him and helped me to go to Mass. I tell you this to show you that no-one looses in respect by sticking up for faith and fatherland, for if a man is unfaithful to either he could not be loyal to you. I stayed in the *J. B. Wood* for a year until I got my arm hurt on a passage from Antwerp to Cardiff where I left her and went home to give my injured arm a rest.

After a month or six weeks rest I started off once more to Glasgow as my jumping-off ground. This time I join a tramp steamer tracking to Spain and North Africa. Her name was the *Vascongada*. After a couple of trips I leave her and join another in the same trade called the *Dunstaffnage,* Captain McKenzie of Dunnet Head (Pentland Firth). I was the favourite with Captain McKenzie, I could do nothing wrong. This was a terrible ship to steer. I was always called to the wheel going in or out of port. All this time nothing happened worth while to record. I stayed in this one until I went home for another holiday. After which, back to Glasgow and joined a boat called the *Emerald* trading to Spain again.

**Certificate of Discharge from the *Vascongada*
for Paddy's second voyage with this vessel**

We made a voyage to Seville and one to Algiers after which we loaded in Grangemouth for Barcelona. Leaving Grangemouth it came down a dense fog as we passed under the Forth Bridge and, while creeping in close off Burntisland trying to pick up the pilot boat, we ran hard on the rocks at the top of high water. That night the *Emerald* broke in two, right amidships. A tug came out and took us off and brought us to the George Hotel, Burntisland. The proprietor was a Mr Wm. Murray, a fine fellow who gave us everything we wanted. We all travelled to Glasgow next day. That was shipwreck number two.

After a week in Glasgow I, with Mick McKeown and several other boys from about home, shipped in a Thompson Liner of Dundee called the *Kildonan¹*. This ship was going right across the Atlantic to a place called Norfolk, Virginia for orders. It was the beginning of December 1896. We had a terrible passage. We met a series of gales. The ship being empty she was tossed about like a balloon on the top of mountainous seas and at the end of 17 days she burst her ballast tanks and drifted onto a sandbank on the Virginian coast (Chesapeake Bay). She went ashore broadside on and listed out towards the Atlantic rollers. So heavy were they over her we couldn't launch our boats. We fired distress rockets and attracted the lifesaving crew who came along in the morning and took us off by a rocket apparatus. This rocket apparatus is a line fired by a gun from the shore. They had some trouble as the ship was about 500 yards off the shore but after many failures they succeeded in landing the lead aboard with the line attached. So we aboard got to work and got it rigged up (some day I'll explain to you how it works. I remember every detail about how to set it up.) We were all taken to the lifesaving station that night and supplied with food and dry clothing.

Next morning when we could see the ship, she had worked over the bank and was close inshore stern-on to the beach. All hands got ready and got on to a buggy and were driven along the sandy beach and put onto the ship again.

This was a week before Christmas. We spent our Christmas there 1896. We rigged up a substitute apparatus from the ship to the shore so that you could go ashore on a 'boson' chair hand over hand. On Christmas eve the steward went ashore thus to secure some turkeys for Christmas dinner. The lifesaving men drove him back to the ship with a hamper of turkeys, chickens and a wee pig. We hauled this up on the line attached to the shore alright, but the steward wouldn't face it himself for the sea was coming rolling in in white foam, so back to the station he went for the night.

Next morning back he came but would not face to come up the line. So the mate came to us and asked for four volunteers to launch a boat to get the steward on board. The sea was so wild he would not order a crew out. I was one of the volunteers and another fellow Willie McAuley of Cushendall. I was on the bow oar. We got ashore alright, got the old steward in the boat, but to get the boat off the beach again was the rub. Every time we got her afloat a wave would lash her back up on the beach. At last I went head over heels into the sea and the boat up on the sand again. When the wave spread up the beach I came up again and sprackled ashore. At last we got the boat afloat and got on board. By this time I was almost frozen into a brass monkey. They put a couple of glasses of brandy into me when I got aboard and by dinner time I was thawed back to life and a Royal Christmas Meal.

Tugs came from New York to tow us off. After eight days they managed to get the ship off. We were towed to Baltimore where she went on dry dock, got a new bottom in there and loaded for London. We were mid-Atlantic homeward on March 17th 1897. Thus I was shipwrecked twice inside one month.

Dad

6

Three times round the Horn

Ravenscliffe Drive

Glasgow

My dear Charles,

I think I may have missed some of my story since my last instalment owing to my having finished my writing pad. I completed, I think, the voyage of the *Kildonan*. Well, Mick McKeown and I made our way to Glasgow and after a trip or two in a tramp ship to Spain and Italy we went home for a holiday. During our stay at home I met another great chum, Jimmy Kane. Mick, if I remember right, remained at home for a long stay so Kane and I set off together and stayed together for a long time. The next year 1898 Kane and I were at home again.

After an enjoyable holiday we set off again for Glasgow. On our way we stayed for a night at the Glasgow Temperance Hotel in Belfast, the proprietor of which belonged to Cushendun (John Morrison). At the hotel, at the same time, was the B-son of a new ship fitting out for her first voyage, the *Rippingham Grange* of London. Mr Morrison got us

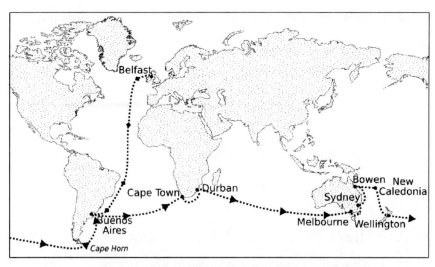

The voyage of the *Rippingham Grange*

persuaded to take a berth in this new liner so we agreed with the boatswain to wait for his ship. She would be ready to sign on in ten days. So back to Cushendun we went for another week and when we returned to Belfast to sign on Kane and I brought another fellow with us from home, by name John O'Neill, who got a berth also. When we had signed on there was a young fellow named Jas McLarty from Layde near Cushendall who was at Hughes Academy in Belfast and who was breaking his heart to get to sea. His father was a road surveyor and a large farmer at Layde.

Our good ship sails from Belfast to Newport, South Wales to load for the River Plate. Going down Belfast Lough, Jim Kane and I were picked out from the crew as quartermasters. This speedy promotion to us two country chaps excited the jealousy of the other members of the sailors who were all Belfast men except O'Neill and the boy McLarty. The crew were nearly all Orangemen. There were 17 firemen all Orangemen except one. There were two RCs among the sailors besides O'Neill, Kane and myself.

The ship loaded at Newport for Insinada, River Plate. From there we loaded mules for South Africa – Cape Town and Durban. While at Cape Town I gathered silver leaves on Table Mountain and had them in a book at home at Chancellor Street for many years. From Cape Town to Durban; from Durban to Melbourne (Australia), Geelong, Sydney, Bowen (Queensland), New Caledonia – a French convict island near where the Japs and Australians are now fighting.

We called in to Wellington on our way east round Cape Horn and with us were seven convicts who stowed away from the island. After we left port they came from their hiding places and worked. They had all our sympathy for they were political prisoners. The ship was to call at Buenos Aires so the evening before we arrived at River Plate the Captain received a message to deliver the convicts on arrival or the whole crew would be interned. During that night the poor fellows were put in irons. They refused to take food. The police boat was waiting for our ship. I actually shed tears when I saw them handed over to the police.

My great chum Jim Kane and I had not been on the best of terms for a little time before this. While at Buenos Aires I met him coming along the deck with tears streaming down his face. I at once went to him and asked him what was wrong. He said he had just got a letter that his mother was dead. My heart went out to him with all my sympathy for I loved the fellow and I knew his kindly mother. We never fell out again.

The Port of Buenos Aires in 1900

We sailed from River Plate for London with a cargo of cattle. We arrived in London in due time. You will be surprised when I tell you that on our arrival in London I was regarded as the 'Hero of the ship'.

I will now tell you how that came about. The bo-son was a bully and could not suffer a sailor to turn the word on him. He put himself out as the light-weight champion of the British Navy where he had been before joining the Merchant service. If weight went by size he was more like the heavy-weight. We were all more or less afraid of him. I was the first who dared to speak back to him. While at boat-drill he tried to show off at my expense in the presence of some passengers. This was too much for my taste. I cut him off by telling him he could show me nothing. He took it bad and picked a row out of me within the next two days. I asked him what he was playing at, if he wanted a row with me. I got as reply a good thump of his heavy-ringed fist. He just lifted the skin of my forehead from my eyebrow to the root of my hair. Instinctively I hit out at him. I spread him on his back across the hatch. I stepped back to let him up. When he got up he jumped at me and got his big arms clasped round my body. He thought by his extra weight he could jam me in a corner but he made a mistake for instead I threw him right over on the broad of his back. By this time I was angry-some. I challenged him to get up and I would fight him with gloves or bare but he stays still. The whole ship's crew were now on the scene. I was now the ship's hero. From that day on he, the bo-son, never dared to give orders or interfere with a quartermaster again. That happened on the passage from South America to Australia.

Before this incident the Belfast crowd used to rag the boy McLarty from Layde, Cushendall. When they went too far I used to take the boy's part. They did not half like it. I let them know that I would not stand by and allow the boy to be made a fool of, besides the lad was a Protestant and I a Catholic from the same district. After the fight with the bo-son the boy McLarty had a good time. No-one tried to rag him again. The news of the bo-son and I reached Belfast before the ship arrived in London. On our arrival at London Jim Kane went to Cushendun to square up over his mother's affairs and I went with him as far as Belfast to stay there until he would return. When we reached Belfast the boy McLarty's father was there to meet us and begged me to go to his place with his son to shoot for a fortnight, but I did not go. He had heard all about my protective interest in his son. Such is the story of my voyage in the liner *Rippingham Grange.*

I stayed in Belfast until Kane came back from Cushendun, then off to Glasgow once more.

P.S. I hope you will not regard this passage as boastful. I often accuse myself of being by nature rather so inclined.

Father.

Ravenscliffe Dr.

Glasgow

My Dear Charles

My story continued from the last instalment.
I will tell you about my best friends at sea and what became of them. I told you in a previous chapter of my companionship with Jim Weldon. How we parted in Cardiff in 1895. We did not meet up again for some years. This is how we met again. I had just arrived in Glasgow after a holiday at home. I got a letter from Weldon that he had arrived in Newcastle in a ship and would like to see me again.

I immediately sent a wire for him to come through to Glasgow. Next evening he arrived. Meantime a Captain McKeegan from near home had offered me a berth in his ship the *Emerald*. I asked the Captain to take Jim Weldon instead of me as I did not wish to leave him in strange lodging after sending for him, assuring Captain McKeegan that Weldon was a better man than I was. The Captain conceded reluctantly but afterwards said that Weldon was the best man he had ever had under him. Jim Weldon was afterwards a captain himself but unfortunately was drowned in Cadiz harbour. He was my first great chum at sea.

How another chum Jim Kane and I separated. In the winter after the voyage in the *Rippingham Grange* we were ashore in Glasgow. I took a severe cold and kept my bed for a few days. Kane went on board an Anchor Liner and got shipped as quartermaster with a captain he had sailed with previously. He tried to get me a berth as quartermaster in the same ship but failed as there were no vacancy as such so we parted at the gangway of the Anchor Liner *Tanai*. By the time Kane's ship came back from New York I was away in an Allan Liner as quartermaster in a ship called the *Sardinian* trading also to New York. The Boer war was brewing at the time. When Kane came back to Glasgow he left the *Tanai* and joined a ship loading horses for South Africa. When his ship arrived at Durban he left the ship and went up to the Transvaal and got a job on the railway where he ultimately became station master at a little place called Boxburgh. He got married to a Dutch girl and lived for many years there. During the last war he joined the South Africa Flying Corps and was for a time in France at the end of which he came to Eastbourne to await transport back to South Africa. While waiting there he made up his mind that he must come to Glasgow to see me.

So to Glasgow he came and stayed with us in Chancellor Street for a week. After his arrival back to his home I heard no word from him for a long time until he was packing up to leave Boxburgh with his family to go to a farm in Rhodesia. While packing thus his wife, who never saw me, picked up an old letter to Jim from me. Jim Kane dropped his packing and wrote me a letter of about six pages. That was his last. I replied to that letter to the address he gave me but I never got an answer. Word of his death came to two retired teachers, cousins of his who lived at Cushendun. That is four years ago. So that is the end of my three great companions at sea. My other great friend Mick McKeown I'm glad to say is still to the fore.

Now to go back to my story. I joined the *Sardinian* trading to New York. On returning from New York, I went a run home while the ship was in Glasgow and stayed a day too long so missed my ship.

So I joined a sailing ship, the famous *Loch Etive* bound for Melbourne. It was October 1900. The captain was a Welshman called Fishwick. The Boer War had just broken

The steamship *Sardinian*

out in 1899. I was the only Irishman in this ship. Most of the crew were Highland men except the captain, second officer, a Russian-finn and myself. We had seven passengers on board.

Just before we sailed the Irish soldiers – especially the Dublin Fusiliers and the Connaught Rangers – so distinguished themselves in beating the Boers at Spion-Kop and making the relief of Ladysmith possible. At the same time at Modder River in the west, the Scots met with a terrible defeat at the hands of the Boers. All Britain was loud in praise of the Irish and I done a fair share of crowing about it to the great annoyance of one Highland man one Alex Robertson of Broadford, Skye. This fellow Robertson and I used to loose the half our watch below arguing about the fighting qualities of our respective countrymen and often loose the whole of our tempers. I was often angry with him. I thought he had no sense of fair play; that he could see no merit in anyone except he wore the kilt but while I would be angry with him, I admired his loyalty to his fellow countrymen. Out of our arguments we came to know each other better and by the time we reached Melbourne Alex Robertson and I were fast friends and remained so ever after. I found him to be a thorough decent fellow. With Alex Robertson I met with a whole colony of Scots people, the finest people I ever met with.

The tug-o-war is worth a mention. It was the mate's watch against the second mate's watch. I was in the latter lot. The mate, who was a Highlander, had all the big hefty Heiland men in his watch. We in the second officer's watch were all lightweights. The third officer was umpire. I was on the tail end of our side. Just at my toes there was a ring-bolt on the deck. The signal goes, we get down to it. The big fellows shift us about a foot but not an inch further. Pull as they might, not a budge could they move us more. What's wrong! The umpire found out. He looked along the line at every man until he came to me. I was sitting on the ring-bolt and had a good hard hold of it with one of my hands underneath my body. "Let go!" he shouted at me. I had to. Oh what! The heavyweights just walked away with us as if we were a lot of empty bags. On New Year's Day they organised another programme of sport that morning. We got Burgare for breakfast and as a protest not a man would turn out for the sports. A breakfast of porage on New Year's Day on a Scottish ship.

The *Loch Etive* was a tidy barque. On the wind few ships could beat her. Running before the wind any ship might do so. We arrive in Melbourne after three and a half months passage. We discharge and load for Hull. During the time we were in Melbourne, Queen Victoria died. The whole city was draped in deep mourning - the Australian people are very loyal to the old country. Melbourne is a splendid city and the people are a grand lot.

The *Loch Etive* at sea

The ship is at last ready for sea again. We sail for home once more. Two of the passengers who went with us were coming home in the ship. Running the Eastern - down to the Horn the weather was very cold and we had very heavy gales of wind - one of these two passengers, a Mr Peacock of Birmingham, was washed overboard at ten o'clock one night as he stept on deck from the stateroom of his mate. A mighty sea swept over the ship at that moment. Nobody knew he was gone until the steward went to call him for breakfast next morning. All hands were deeply sorry for his loss. He was such a good fellow. He used always to give us a hand to pull round the yards. At the time Mr Peacock was washed overboard we were nearing Cape Horn. The night the *Loch Etive* rounded the Horn the sea was as smooth as a lake except for the great everlasting swell that rolls from west to east forever. This is my third time around Cape Horn and I think my last time.

When we arrive in the Channel a baffering calm falls around the ship and for a day we drift about with the tide. This is anything but pleasant as everyone is longing to get ashore. At last we arrive in Hull after a passage of 115 days from Melbourne. The first thing the crew do is make a beeline for the nearest restaurant and order ham and eggs and plenty of it. After three and a half months picking moths out of our biscuits, I never got such a starving as I did in the *Loch Etive* on the passage home. From we left Melbourne until we arrived in Hull, I never ate a biscuit but what I had to split and pick out the moths. The crew of the *Loch Etive* is paid off at Hull and most of us take the train for Glasgow. Robertson went home to Skye and I to Ireland.

7

Brooklyn and Marriage

On my return to Glasgow I join the *Sardinian* once more for New York. It was July 1901. While at New York I visited all my old friends in Greenpoint, Brooklyn. I called to see an old neighbour of ours who was born and reared beside me in Dunouragan, Mary McCormick (better known as Mary Roe), and who had become the second wife of Robert McElheran. Robert McElheran was my future father-in-law although I little dreamed at the time that I would become his son-in-law. When I returned from New York I went for a short holiday to Cushendun while my ship was in Glasgow.

The evening after I arrived home I was going into Mrs O'Connor's in Straid (Mick McKeown's aunt) when James McCart and Susannah were passing with a cart on their way to Cushendall to meet Mamie (your mother) who was coming down from Ballymena for a lint-pulling which McCart was to have on the Monday following. James McCart and his wife (Robert McElheran's sister) had come to Ireland for a holiday from Brooklyn meaning to go back to the States and brought with them their niece Mary McElheran whose mother was dead. Instead of returning to America, Mr McCart bought a

New York harbour from the Brooklyn Bridge, 1907

farm at Cushendun and settled down and Miss McElheran remained with them. Mr McCart had heard I was in New York so both he and Susanna (another sister of Bob McElheran) were very anxious to hear all about Bob and his wife.

I met your mother for the first time next day at the chapel and she, hearing that I had been in New York and had met her father, was naturally anxious to see me and hear how her father was doing, as he had married again. That same evening she met my brother Jim and asked him to be sure to bring me with him to the dance the next night in McCart's house after the lint-pulling. So that's how we met.

I did not tarry long at home as I wished to be in time to catch the *Sardinian* before she sailed from Glasgow. Mick and I set off from home for the city on the Clyde. The 1900

Exhibition was in full swing in Glasgow at the time. For a week, with some friends from home who were out for the Exhibition, McKeown and I had a great time.

Mick and I joined the *Sardinian* again for New York. As usual we fall out on the way. When we arrive in New York, I go again to Greenpoint, Brooklyn to see the 'natives'. Mary Roe and some friends persuaded me to leave the ship and go bar-tending with a Mrs McIlroy who had a saloon and whose husband had died recently. I left the ship after leaving a message with Mick to put my clothes ashore at Glasgow. So off I go to make my fortune sloshing beer across. The bar-tending I soon got sick of and after three weeks I quit. I went to stay with Mrs Bob McElheran - better known as 'Mary Roe' who had been my next door neighbour at home in Ireland before she went to New York and became the second wife of Captain Bob McElheran. He was a captain on the Standard Oil boats he spoke for me to get a job on the lighters. After a few days I got a start piling case-oil on lighters. It was murder. The men here in Britain know nothing about hard work. John D. Rockafeller, the owner of Standard Oil of America, made his fabulous wealth on the blood and sweat of men. Did it make him happy? No, it worried him into a life of misery and dread. But to get back to my story, I stuck it for a year. By that time I was getting expert at my work. I was never such a man as I was then although the work was hard. I was well fed and went to bed early.

During the time I was thus employed I kept in regular correspondence with Mary McElheran. By mutual consent we regarded one another as engaged without any formal ceremony about it. So at the end of May 1902 I gave notice that I was leaving the Standard Oil.

Dad

✷

Ravenscliffe Dr

Glasgow

My Dear Charles

The head man over me was a Swede called Andersen. When I told him I was leaving to go to Ireland he got quite earnest in his appeal not to leave – that I was first on the list for a steady job for life (mate then captain) on the lighters. He gave me three days to reconsider my decision. I did not tell him my reason for leaving but had he been able to offer me the Presidency of the United States I would have refused for I had made up my mind that I would return and marry Mamie.

That night I told big Bob (your grandfather) what I intended to do – that I was leaving and why. He gave me his blessing and also told me that he knew for some time before that my name was first on the list for a permanent position on the Standard Oil but did not mention it to me. He told me further that when he spoke for me at first for a start if there was any vacancy, that he did not know whether I could work or not, but if I could not to throw me out. Now of all the things he could have done to me or for me I could not have wished for better for it was always repugnant to me to think that I was leaning on anyone. Anyway I didn't let him down.

About the end of May 1902 I left New York in a Red Star Liner called the *Kensington Star* bound for Antwerp (Belgium). From there I came to Glasgow by Leith and proceeded straight to Ballymena where Mamie was living with her uncle and aunt, Mr and Mrs McCart. Strange to say, Mamie and I were both bashful lovers. She was modest and reserved by nature. I, although thrown among rough men for years through the world, felt as bashful as a schoolgirl in the company of women.

However we managed to get engaged and arranged to get married as soon as possible. So on July 2nd 1902 your mother and I were married by the late Very Rev Father McMullan P.P.V.F. in All Saints Church, Ballymena. After a short honeymoon to Belfast, Bangor, Larne and Portrush we went back to Ballymena. There I spent a good long holiday of two months between Ballymena, Barromean farm in Cushendun which belonged to Mr McCart and Susannah's at Straid. As your mother was the only help her aunt had in Ballymena I thought I would go to sea again for a time. The night I started off to go to Glasgow Mamie went with me to

Paddy and Mamie Murray

the station. I got my ticket for Belfast and we stood and waited for the train. For some reason or other the train did not come until long after the time to catch the boat. So back we went to Mrs McCart. When she saw us, and not knowing the real cause, she said, "I knew she wouldn't let you go!".

Next night I went off and this time the train turned up in time. Next day I met an old friend in Glasgow - Captain William Kane - who asked me if I would go with him on a coaster called the *Deania* which he was master of. The boat was going to Glenarm (on the Antrim coast) the next morning to load limestone. So I joined the *Deania* and arrived in Glenarm on Sunday morning. We had on board a boy's bicycle to be left in Glenarm. On Sunday afternoon I felt very lonely aboard so I took out the bicycle and started off for Ballymena 20 miles distant. There had been a deluge of rain over the weekend and the roads were torn up with the floods. I had to walk up the mountain road and push the bicycle for about four miles. I heard a washer fall off the crank of the wheel and looking round I saw that one of the pedals was gone. I turned down the road again to search for it. Some distance down the road among the rough stony surface I found the pedal, but the nut was lost. I went to a farmhouse in search of a nut but couldn't find one, so I tied a strong string on it outside the pedal for a nut and made the rest of the journey on the boy's bicycle. When I arrived in Ballymena my wife and her aunt thought I fell from the clouds for I was only three days away.

Next morning I left early to catch the *Deania* before she sailed from Glenarm, but I was about ten minutes too late. As I reached Glenarm she was just passing out from the pier and I felt very much that I looked like a half-shut knife because the bicycle was far too short for me. The captain had left word for me to cross in a puffer that was leaving Glenarm later. So I caught the *Deania* next evening in Glasgow. I stay with the *Deania* for a few months then I have another holiday in Ballymena at the end of which I go back to Glasgow.

There I join the *Fernside* trading to Spain, Italy, Algiers and Glasgow. I was ploughing through the Gulf of Lyons bound for Genoa at the moment May was born. Before leaving Genoa I received a letter from your mother – a line saying these words, "I am lying here in bed with the loveliest baby girl in the world by my side. We are both well." I think it was the happiest moment of my whole life for I was anxious about her for long before. The next thrill of supreme happiness was coming home from the Samaritan Hospital the Sunday after your mother went through her operation. I went to see her on the Saturday. She seemed all out. I asked Sister if I could see mother on the Sunday. She said I could call and if she was then well enough to see anyone I might get in. I called and got to see her. She was so much improved I could hardly believe my eyes.

I came home that evening in the tramcar. I felt overjoyed. I can't remember any such joyous moments in my life although I have had, thank God, a fairly happy life and often thank God for such gifts as the family he in his goodness has given me and I often have thought, and do think myself, so unworthy of such gifts. I can only lay claim to one virtue to merit such favours – my love of Mass, not only on Sunday but on all days of the week when I could and I can't forget for a moment that it was God's gift to me for I know in myself I am as weak as the least of men.

I came home to Glasgow in the *Fernside*, paid off and made my way to Ballymena to see my baby and her mother.

After that I have a couple of trips on the *Leila* to Spain. When May was 7 months old I brought your mother to Glasgow meaning to go to sea again but Mamie would not have it so. If I couldn't get a job ashore she would go back to her aunt and uncle. So the only thing I could think of was something connected with shipping. Therefore to the dock I turned and joined the Dockers' Union.

I went to the Anchor Line to seek a job. I knew no-one there. I asked a man who I saw was a boss if he could give me a start.

"Where do you belong?" he asked me.

"I am an Irishman," I replied.

"No use," he said, "We have too many Irishmen about here already." So I passed on. This man was a head foreman but not the only one. About a week later I happened to get started by a foreman called William Gibson. It was on an Anchor Line ship, the *Ethiopia* just arrived from New York. It was a nightshift. We start at 6 o'clock at night and we work all night and at 6 in the morning the crowd works on all morning. So do I. That was 24 hours in a truck up and down a stage. I felt pretty tired at the end of the second shift. This was the general mode of work at the dock at the time to make a living. Other times you might be idle for days at a time. I hated it but I had no choice. Had it not been for the fact that I had little money I couldn't have stuck it. I started in the dock in October 1903 in the stevedore department. Such was my beginning at the Anchor Line.

8

Docks, politics and family

Times was very bad; one would be lucky to average 3 days a week. I worried a lot about how I would support a family if God willed it so. For nearly three and a half years I worked like this - often 36 consecutive hours when I got a chance to do so and glad of the opportunity.

About the first working day after New Year 1908 I was working at one of the company ships loading for Calcutta. It was bitter cold with a dense fog on the Clyde and the ground thickly covered with white frost. The time was about 5.30pm. There were a large crowd of men gathering looking for nightshift. I was working taking barrels of pitch from the pierhead opposite the ship. Suddenly I heard a commotion alongside the ship's bow. Something wrong. I ran across to see a man in the water. Hugh Hillan, the head foreman, was calling excitedly if someone would try and save the man. There were about 200 men around him when I arrived. All were anxious to save the man but would not venture as it was low water at the time and no-one could see him in the fog. They could only hear him splashing and gurgling. "I'll go down on a rope," I said.

Half-a-dozen men got a sodden rope that was lying on the quay and I slid down into the murky water, the men on the quay holding onto the end. I got hold of the man, held his head up with one hand and myself with the other until the men got a ladder from the ship. They got a ladder but it was too short. It wouldn't come halfway down to me. They had to go to the ship again for a long ladder. All this time I was holding the man and myself from drowning for I could not swim a stroke. When the long ladder came I shoved one leg through the rungs which enabled me to have the use of both hands. The men ashore threw the end of a heaving line, the end of which I bent round under the armpit of the man then told them to pull him gently up while I held his face clear of the quay wall and climbed the ladder at the same time. When I got on to the wharf a rush was made for me everybody wanted to shake hands with me. My own foreman and the head foreman got round me. The foreman forced money on me to go over to Kelvinhaugh for brandy for myself. Meanwhile other men carried the man into the pilothouse to await the ambulance.

This happened on a Friday night. Next day I was sent for to go before the superintendent who promoted me foreman - I, the unknown stranger of three years before. I went to see the man I saved next day in the Western Infirmary. He spoke to me freely and thanked me. Twenty minutes after I left him he died. His name was John Duff of Islandmagee, Co Antrim.

This account of my sea life and my entry on to land life may seem slightly boastful. It's not – what I write is just the facts as they happened. The promotion that I have mentioned I can truly say I was promoted on the 'field'. I did not ask for it, besides there were several other applicants with someone behind them already in. I was indeed very proud and thankful to get it. It was a godsend for there were several years of bad times followed.

Dad

*

Ravenscliffe Dr.

Glasgow

My Dear Charles

I have already mentioned at the outset I worried about the support of a large family. Well, every additional child God gave to us He also gave us more to feed and clothe them. We first lived at 48 Blackburn Street, Plantation in St Margaret's Parish where Jack was born. Next at 78 McLean Street (same parish) where Jim and Kathleen (Ena) was born. During the summer of 1908 my wife, who wasn't keeping in very good health went to Ireland for a time to see if it would improve her health. I went to stay with my sister Mrs Mary Ann Lawn. Thus we lived for over a year. Meantime the Anchor Line was soon to shift their berth from Stobcross Quay to the new wharf at Yorkhill, which they did early in 1910. That same spring I took a house at 112 Dumbarton Road where Josephine was born and where my beloved daughter Ena died. The death of this child at the age of three and a half years was the greatest sorrow of my life. After about 18 months we moved to 9 India Street (now 69 Chancellor Street) where we lived for over twenty years and where you were born and also Patsy, Eileen and Frank.

Paddy and Mamie with five of their family

The next year 1911 the sailors strike broke out. At this time the dockers were disorganised. They had no leader. At the end of the sailors strike they adopted a man named Joe Houghton as their leader and started to reorganise. This man Houghton was a shoemaker by trade so knew nothing about dock work. The extreme element did not forget to prompt him in all the wild demands they desired and Houghton did not hesitate to give it voice. Hundreds flocked into the new Union at 1/- a head. In a short time there were between 3000 and 4000 men in the new Scottish Union of Dockers.

At first the demands of the men were reasonable and met with success, but as time went on their demands increased until they did not know when to stop. Then the men clamoured for the foremen to join the Union and on the 5th October 1911 sent delegates round the docks to warn all foremen to be in the Union by 9 o'clock the next morning and that the entrance fee would be 15/-. If by 9 o'clock they were not joined up the fee would be raised to one pound. Otherwise no man would be allowed to work with them and foremen when in the Union would be guaranteed their jobs whether the masters liked it or not. In short, if they joined the Union they would be kept in their jobs, but if not they would be driven out of their positions.

"Is that your terms?" I asked the two men who came to the Anchor Line.

"Yes," they replied.

"Then you can tell the Union officials to go to Hell," I said, "as far as I'm concerned." Before I would stoop to such terms I would go and eat grass first. All our foremen, 19 in number, held a meeting that night. I put my views before them and all approved of my action.

Next morning 6th October a strike was called until we joined the Union. The same night the Anchor Line sent the £19 to the Union for their 19 foremen without asking our permission to do so. The company did this in order to sail their mail boat which was held up. The morning after, the 7th October, Joe Houghton came with a great crowd to the Anchor Line gate and haranged the crowd in a fiery speech against sailor Murray who he dubbed as the leader of the foremen at the Anchor Line. As all the foremen in the Harbour had come in peaceably, the foremen at the Anchor Line would have done the same had it not been for sailor Murray. Further, that I harassed the men under me and bullied them and other unfair acts, and finally proposed to drive me out of my job altogether. When the meeting was over I saw two of my fellow foremen coming from the speech. They were talking in angry tones.

"What's up?" I asked them.

"Oh, about what that scoundrel said about you," they said.

"About me?" I said.

"Yes," said Willie Grigson, "he said all sorts of lies about you" – telling me what Houghton had said. Knowing that I never done to a man under my charge a dishonest act to my knowledge, I there and then rushed outside the gate into the middle of the crowd and challenged any man to say if I ever done a dishonourable act to anyone to step into the ring and give the proof. Three times I demanded but nobody came forward. At last a man named John Curren stept into the centre and said he knew me ever since I became a foreman and never knew me to do any man but what was upright and just. I then rushed up to the office where Joe Houghton and his bodyguard were waiting. I challenged him to come down to the crowd he had addressed and prove his statements but no, he would not face the music.

I afterwards wrote demanding an apology from Houghton. Instead of receiving an apology I received a summons to appear before a committee of the Union in their head office at Oswald Street to explain myself to the Union as I had ignored the Anchor Line's act in paying the £1 entrance fee. They had done it for their own purpose to let their ship sail. I also ignored the Union for three years, during which time I endured much persecution from the agents of the Union. At the end of three years, on the friendly invitation of the chairman (B. Havlin) of the committee I joined the Union of my own free will and paid my own entrance fee. On the night I joined I presented this note to the committee: "I have come to join your Union of my own free will with an understanding that, in the execution of my duties as a foreman, I shall suffer no interference." These conditions were accepted with open arms. Otherwise I would have walked out.

Five years after I became a 'gaffer' I was a leading foreman. I, at that time, could do what I liked – pretty well. I could get almost anybody a job there I wished – until I got too big for my boots. I refused the orders of my superior one day in 1921 and was reported to the super. I was too proud to apologise and got what I highly deserved - the 'sack'. It was a terrible drop and I felt it some. It was a sensation in Glasgow harbour. 'Sailor' Murray being sacked from the mail boats.

Just about the same time a publican friend came to Partick and asked me to apply for a pub licence – that my name was good in Glasgow and I could get as much money as I wished, £6000 if I wanted to buy a pub. He left me a time to think it over. I told mother, I told Jack and I told our friend Dr Hendry about it. All were anxious that I should. I thought it over long and hard. I finally decided I wouldn't. Instead I just put off my coat, rolled up my sleeves and went to work and work hard. Today I am thankful that I did what I did.

One night Jack spoke to me and said, "Da, why not take the great offer that your friend made to you?"

I replied, "I did not like the trade."

He said, "Well, you can't cure the evils that's in it by staying out of it."

"No," I said, "but suppose we have a pub, and you and I are in the bar on a Saturday. We have everything ready. We see three men coming home from work. They come in for a drink. The first man calls a drink for himself and his two friends. They drink each other's health, and the second man stands his turn. Now they begin to talk freely and the third man stands his turn. By this time the drink affects the men. They begin to boast and very likely will call for more until they become the worse for drink. All this time we (Jack and I) serve them and take their money. At the same time their wives and children are looking for them coming home with the money that was much needed for food and clothing. While this was going on we were growing rich on the poverty and sorrow of many women and children. Would you like that way of making a living?" Jack never mentioned the subject again.

I had quite a hard time following that episode. A bad time spread over the world after the last war. I worked thus for eight years. When I met the man who sacked me I passed him with my head in the air. At the same time I had no resentment against him for I felt that he only done to me what I would have done to him, had I been in his place and he in mine if he refused my orders. One morning I was passing through the Anchor Line shed. There were many men idle, I among them. My old superior saw I was left. He rushed after me and asked me if I would take a job in the store for a day or two. I said I would as I was there for work.

During the course of the day he came into the store to me. I asked him if it was true that he was soon to retire from the Anchor Line. He said it was quite true. I said to him that I

Queen's Dock, Glasgow

was very sorry to hear that he was leaving the company. He replied that what made him sorry was what happened between him and me. I said to him not to let that trouble him for he never done anything to me but what I deserved for indeed never did any man do more kindness or trust me as he did and I spoke the truth. There is nothing that happened during my time with the Anchor Line that I regret more than the impudence and defiance that I showed to that man for he was an honest, god-fearing man. His name was Dougal MacGilvray. He died in Tiree about six years ago. I am glad to say I wrote to him when I heard he was ill. He replied to my letter in the most warm and friendly manner thanking me for my letter. Before he left the Anchor Line he begged me to go back as foreman which I confess I was glad to accept. It was also a sensation in the harbour when I was reinstated at the

Anchor Line as there was quite a crowd in for the vacancy, most of them Freemasons and men with some push to them but I got the job and I thanked God for it and also for the check I got to my pride. A drop down the 'ladder' is good for us when we get too hot.

I remained in the company until it was sold out five years ago when all the staff, except a few in high places, had to leave by reason that the new company contracted out our department. I could be foreman in to other companies since if I wished but I don't wish it. I just want to be free to go and come as I like.

Well, I'll give you some of the incidents and a few thrills of my life and times in Partick. I will not give you much in this instalment. We went to live in Partick in 1910. I soon became well known. On the first day I went to Partick I met Dean McNairney on the street. I saluted him as I would any priest. He stopped me and asked in a very friendly way what I was looking for. I told him a house. He warned me where to avoid. He kept his eye on me after. On my first Sunday at St Peter's he caught me in the porch going in and would have me join the St Vincent de Paul Conference and would take no denial. Coming out he rushed me over to the girls' school where the conference were being held and where I had the privilege of meeting some of the best men I ever met during my lifetime, men indeed it was an honour to associate with in a noble work. Canon McNairney and I became great friends.

Some short time afterwards I was invited to join the United Irish League. There too I became an active member. The following October the U.I.L. Branch nominated seven members for the Partick East Ward Committee. This is a local municipal body to advise the town councillors representing the district. There were about 40 candidates for 14 seats. All seven of us got elected and I at the top of the poll. This was a surprise to me for the big gun P.J. O'Callaghan was one of the seven of us nominated. I being at the top I was elected for three years, the middle section for two years and the lot at the lower end for one year. Before my three year term was up the Great War broke out during which period there were no elections in Glasgow so I remained in until 1921 when there were General Elections of all municipal bodies.

I will tell you in my next instalment all about the election of 1921. It proved to be the greatest thrill of my life in Partick so just wait till you get it.

Cheerio.

Dad

✳

End of the letters

9

Paddy's son Frank

Here end the letters. They had been written from Ravenscliffe Drive in Giffnock – a well-to-do suburb of Glasgow to which my grandparents had moved after my grandfather's retiral. However they stayed in Giffnock for only a very short time as they, particularly my grandmother, missed the neighbourliness and the hubbub of life in Partick near the docks and so moved back there.

The son next to Charlie in age was Frank. Frank had no academic aspirations and in the 1930s was desperate to leave school and work in the docks but his father would not hear of it. Paddy himself was working as a foreman at the docks at the time but saw education as an opening up of opportunities for his family. Eventually Paddy relented and Frank had his wish. He was employed in John Brown's shipyard building the *Queen Mary*. He remained at the docks for about ten years ostensibly to become a sheet metal worker but for a long time at the start was a 'tea-boy'.

During his time there he had an unhappy and short-lived marriage. When his marriage ended Frank emigrated to New York and settled in Greenpoint, Brooklyn where the family connections were. He worked in the Brooklyn docks for a while but increasingly felt that, due to the impetuosity of youth, he had left school prematurely. He enrolled in evening classes at the Pratt Institute where he obtained a qualification in engineering. On the final night at the Pratt Institute Frank, as the student representative, gave a farewell speech. I include his speech here as it evokes the atmosphere of the Clydeside docks at the time his father Paddy also worked there.

"This is the last night at the Pratt Institute for some of us here. With the grace of God and the grades of Mr Oakes I hope that it will be my last night, and that I will graduate in July. Tonight I would like to give you some background on the reason why I came to the Pratt Institute.

I obviously did attend the Institute to learn something. The real reason goes away back to the time I wanted to leave High School.

In Scotland where I went to school, you could go through three years of high school, sit for the Day School Certificate and leave, or continue through six years of High School, sit for the Higher Leaving Certificate and if successful you could enter a university or if you didn't want to go to a university you were at least better prepared for the better jobs.

I had got the Day School Certificate at the end of my third year and I wanted to leave school. I asked my father but he didn't want to hear anything about it. If I had no foresight at least my parents had some and for a very good reason.

The year was 1933 and the Depression was on at that time as we all know or have at least heard. The City of Glasgow where I lived is, or was at that time, a centre of shipbuilding and heavy engineering. You can well imagine the chances of employment in a city like that where the economy of the population was geared to such a limited scope of industry.

Every street corner yielded evidence of the Depression. Thousands upon thousands of tradesmen of all sorts hanging around with nothing to do. In 1932 all the shipyards where work had not already stopped were closed down and a blight descended on the area. Everywhere you looked along the waterfront you could see ships in various stages of completion lying rusting in their stocks.

I lived near the yard where the *Queen Mary* was being built, and it was sad to see her huge hull, which dwarfed all else around, stand silent and rusting. As you passed the yard you could see her prow rise almost to the clouds. She seemed to stand about ten miles high. Fantastic stories circulated about her appointments, not officially circulated, but imagination amongst the young had run riot. She was to have devices that I'm sure man will never get around to inventing for another hundred years.

But to get back down off the *Queen Mary*. I was most unhappy at school. One reason for this was because my own brother taught at the same school. This was most embarrassing to me, and it was most embarrassing to him I can tell you. Another reason was because I couldn't possibly see how I could be taught anything, I was that clever I knew everything there was to know.

The *Queen Mary* under construction

In 1934 the government gave out some kind of low interest loans to help industry and work was resumed on the *Queen Mary* and on some other ships. This was a great relief - it didn't solve the employment problem but it was a start.

Men returned to work in the yards and the noise of the riveters, caulkers and blacksmiths seemed like music. The clamour and the smoke of the yards held a great attraction for me. By this time I had finished my fourth year at High School and I wanted more than anything to work in the shipyards.

Again I approached my father about leaving school, and again he wouldn't listen. Eventually he did relent, and told me that once I had surrendered my parasitical status in the home, I had lost it for good; there could be no second chance at school.

That was enough for me. All I needed was to get a job and I would soon tell him how good I was. I was fortunate enough to land a job in John Brown's shipyard where the *Queen Mary* was being built. I was interviewed with a few other youths of my own age, and after a little pep talk by the personnel manager about the wonderful opportunity we were being given and slogans such as:

'We shall build good ships
At a profit if we can
At a loss if we must
But always good ships'

Papers were signed, and for the next five years I was to be an apprentice sheet metal worker. I had a strange idea of what an apprenticeship in the shipyards entailed although I had had every chance to know what it was like from boys of my own age who had already started on theirs. I had thought of an apprenticeship in terms of being articled to some great master like a Stradivarius where the pupil would watch the master's every move, and the master would watch the pupil's every move. But I was soon to be disillusioned. I soon found out that the master was the nearest journeyman who had just run out of cigarettes and wanted some quick, or who decided he wanted a can of tea made. This lasted for a couple of months; at that time it seemed to me an eternity. I remember one day being depressed about the situation but I resigned myself to the fact that although I knew nothing about the building of ships, I was one terrific tea maker. After a few months I got wise to the fact that I wasn't supposed to run any errands and that the men were supposed to be teaching me all the rudiments of sheet metal work. By this time I had been well sorry I had left school.

I didn't see the devotion to work or the pride in work I had anticipated. In fact, I didn't see much work, at least, not commensurate with the noise and smoke I had noticed from outside the yard. But somehow or other ships did get built, and as time progressed I acquired a certain amount of skill. In 1936 the *Queen Mary* was ready and the keel of the *Queen Elizabeth* was laid. About this time I had settled down to making what seemed to be endless miles of sheet metal ventilating ducts. I used to wonder if there were enough people in the world to breathe all the air these ducts could carry. But later still the work became more challenging and diversified. But working on ships in the early stages of construction through the chill and frost of the long winters which we had could never convince me I had done the right thing by leaving school when I had a chance to stay on and I think I was quite convinced that I wasn't as clever as I had thought, but there was no turning back.

Frank Murray

I said earlier that I had noticed a lack of pride, but that's not exactly true. We did have pride. There existed somewhat the same strong nationalism like that we have here in America. Perhaps not so strong or perhaps with not so much justification. But everything we had or made was the biggest in the world, the best in the world, the fastest in the world and so on. There is no harm in these fancies, rather there is some good, especially if they reconcile people to their lot. I had started off earning 2 dollars a week in my first year and my pay increased by leaps and bounds to the staggering figure of 8 dollars a week in my fifth year.

Sometimes on my way home from work after being paid I would examine these claims to greatness. There was no doubt we were building the biggest ships in the world, they could be the best and the fastest in the world, but when I looked at my pay I was certain that they must surely be the cheapest in the world.

My five years eventually came to an end and in 1939 I became a fully fledged sheet metal worker. Not without some pride but with a great deal of regret. The usual procedure with an employer up to that time was to work a youth through a five-year apprenticeship, then employ him for another year as an improver at a reduced journeyman rate, then to lay him off to join the countless others unemployed. But this was 1939 and employers could no longer get away with that, the Second World War was coming.

But in normal times the future was really bleak. You'll find this fairly general in Europe – between the ages of 19 and 21 your life is more or less fashioned, by that age you have set the pattern for your life. With few exceptions there is no second chance as far as education goes. Very rarely do you get a chance to go to a college or university like you do in the United States, and that is why I came to the US and saw that I still had a second chance. I grasped at it with both hands because here was a chance that I would probably never get anywhere else. I hope you all realize this. I know you are all going to some inconvenience to attend the institute, but I hope you know that this is probably the only place in the world where you would get the chance, notwithstanding your willingness to sacrifice something.

I've seen people come and go at Pratt, not all lasted the pace. If I hadn't been so clever in 1934 when I thought I knew everything, I wouldn't be marching down to Pratt Institute on these warm nights humbly trying to learn something."

Learn something he did. The qualification Frank gained in engineering enabled him to aspire to a higher ranking job with the Cunard Line.

Meantime his father Paddy stayed in Partick in Glasgow with many of his family nearby. After he retired from his job as foreman at the docks in 1937, he remained involved in church and local politics, his family and friends and frequent trips to Cushendun in Ireland. Mamie, his wife, died in 1947 age 67.

In 1949 he spent three months in America between his daughter Josie's home in Connecticut and his son Frank's house in Greenpoint, Brooklyn. In a letter home, just after arriving, his father remarks "Frank has a good job and everybody seems to love him. He is the best improved boy I ever saw". The summer nights at the Pratt Institute were not in vain!

It had been almost half a century since Paddy had spent a year living and working in Brooklyn (Chapter 7). Greenpoint was also where his wife had been reared and where many immigrants from his native land had settled. During this visit to Brooklyn in a letter he sent to his oldest son Jack in Glasgow he wrote "I did expect to meet many old friends in

Greenpoint. But there's such a crowd of friends who has gathered around me here. To cut the story short, if any of the Hollywood stars come to Brooklyn, and wishes to be known, they will require to go on the waiting list until I leave. I have three different parties to attend this week all got up for me. I shall be glad when I get back to Josie for a week or two of peace."

✳

Two years later in 1952 at the age of 80 my grandfather returned to the USA. This time he travelled on the *Queen Mary* (to the building of which his son Frank had contributed!). As he stood on the deck doffing his hat little could his fellow passengers guess that their travelling companion had, on previous crossings of the Atlantic, clambered up riggings and clung to yardarms of gale-tossed ships; that his first landing on American soil had been via a rope attached to his ship, wrecked on the Virginian coast.

In a letter home from the States on this visit, he expressed mild irritation at his daughter Josie's anxiety as he ventured out on his own. "She fusses over me like I am a baby. I tell her I have travelled all over the world and not got lost."

Patrick Murray died in his bed in Glasgow on the 24th June 1956 and was buried in Cushendun in the Glens of Antrim, less than a mile from his birthplace.

**Paddy Murray aboard R.M.S. *Queen Mary*, bound for
New York**

List of Voyages

Drumaderry 1891   Belfast – Glasgow

Mandarin   1891   Troon – La Rochelle – Santander – Glasgow

Mandarin   1891   Glasgow – La Rochelle – Bilbao – Glasgow

Cherokee   1891   Glasgow – Tobermory - Stornoway – Thurso – Glasgow

Germina   1891   Glasgow – Cardiff

True Britain 1891   Cardiff – Bordeaux - Bilbao – Cardiff

Alfred Ray   12/08/91 - 3/12/91 Cardiff – Portsmouth – Seaham – Portsmouth – Cardiff [for a number of trips]

Loch Gair   1892   Glasgow – Loch Etive – Portree – Belfast

Lively Lass   1892   Glasgow - West of Ireland

Loch Gair   1892   Glasgow – Loch Etive – Skye - Belfast

Exit   1892   Glasgow – Loch Etive [Shipwrecked]

Norma   1893   Glasgow – Newport – via Azores/ Equator – Rio de Janeiro [mutinied and left ship]

Mylomene   09/10/93 - 12/06/94 Rio de Janeiro – Adelaide – New Zealand – via Cape Horn – London

Ruperra   26/06/94 - 24/08/94 Cardiff – Selonica, Black Sea – Cork – Cardiff

J. B .Wood   10/09/94 - 10/08/95 Cardiff – Galway – Antwerp – Cardiff

Vascongada   02/10/95 – 22/11/95 Glasgow – Spain – North Africa – Glasgow

Vascongada   24/11/95 - 28/12/95   [as above]

Dunstaffnage   17/02/96 - 26/06/96   [as above]

Emerald   30/09/96 - 20/11/96 Glasgow – Seville – Algiers – Grangemouth – Burntisland [shipwrecked]

Kildona	**Nov1896 - April 1897**	Glasgow – Chesapeake Bay, Virginia USA [shipwrecked: towed to Baltimore dry dock for three months] – London
Klyde	**27/04/98 - 24/05/98**	Glasgow – Spain – Ardrossan
Merannio	**31/05/98 - 22/07/98**	Ardrossan – Italy – Troon
Rippingham Grange	**1898 – 1899**	Belfast – Newport – Insinada, River Plate – Cape Town Durban – Melbourne – Geelong – Sydney – Bowen – New Caledonia – Wellington (NZ) – round Cape Horn – Buenos Aires – London – Belfast
Cragoswald	**06/06/99 - 28/09/99**	Glasgow – Karachi – South Shields [this voyage is not mentioned in his letters but in his Discharge Book]
Loch Etive	**12/10/1900 - 28/06/01**	Glasgow – Melbourne - Hull
Sardinian	**06/07/01 - 05/08/01**	Glasgow – New York – Glasgow
Sardinian	**14/09/01 -**	Glasgow – New York [voyage not completed]

[Worked for one year for Standard Oil on lighters in Brooklyn Harbour, New York]

Kensington	**May 1902**	New York – Antwerp
Deania	**Sept 1902**	Glenarm – Glasgow – Glenarm [for a few months]
Fernside	**19/02/03 - 02/05/03**	Glasgow – Spain – Italy – Algiers – Newport
Leila	**16/06/03 - 07/07/03**	Glasgow – Spain – Ardrossan
Leila	**09/07/03 - 06/09/03**	[as above]

Notes on ships mentioned

Name	Reg. No.	Type of Ship	Port of Registry	Where built	Year	Tons	Owner	Notes
Drumaderry								
Mandarin	84289	Iron	Glasgow	Paisley	1881	387	Alexander A Wyllie, Troon	
Cherokee	52136	Schooner	Newry	Bay Verte, N.B.	1865	77	A. Nickle, Larne	Wrecked near Stranraer, Dec. 1891
Germina of Arklow		Three-masted schooner		Harland & Wolff, Belfast ?	1874?			
True Briton	83825	Iron	Cardiff	Palmers, Newcastle	1881	987	Gibbs & Lee, Cardiff	Sank off Yarmouth, 1953
Alfred Ray	17436	Brigantine	Portsmouth	Littlehampton	1857	192	J. T. Crampton, Landport	A hulk in Portsmouth, 1900

Name	Reg. No.	Type of Ship	Port of Registry	Where built	Year	Tons	Owner	Notes
Loch Gair	96006	Iron	Glasgow	Bowling	1897	46	John G. Stewart, Glasgow	
Lively Lass	9272 or 38884	Schooner			1851			
Exit	54260	Schooner	Campbeltown	Prince Edward I.	1866	100	Donald Blair, Campbeltown	Lost off Connel, July 1892
Norma	98433	Barque	Cardiff	Whiteinch	1893	1999	M. J. Begg, Cardiff	Sank at Port Adelaide after collision, Apr 1907
Mylomene	86157	3-masted ship	Liverpool		1882	1900	David Fernie, Liverpool	Hulk at Vancouver, 1903
Ruperra	87487	Iron	Cardiff	Jarrow	1883	200	John Cory, Cardiff	
J.B. Wood	66411	Brigantine	Newport	Prince Edward I.	1873	128	James Pollard	
Vascongada	95011	Steel	Glasgow	A Stephen, Glasgow	1887	1483	Reid & Ferguson	Sank after collision, 1918

Name	Reg. No.	Type of Ship	Port of Registry	Where built	Year	Tons	Owner	Notes
Dunstaffnage	104568	Steel	Glasgow	Mackie & Thomson, Govan	1894	1393	Smith Steamship Co., Glasgow	Ran aground N. of Flamborough Head, Oct 1908
Emerald	2649		Glasgow			567	Donald & Taylor, Glasgow	Lost off Burntisland, Nov. 1896
Kildona	93769	Steel	Dundee	T. Royden, Liverpool		3582	W Thompson & Sons, Dundee	Lost off Nova Scotia, 1907
Klyde	86985	Iron	Glasgow	Swan Hunter, Wallsend	1897	992	Maclay & McIntyre, Glasgow	Wrecked at Istanbul, Jan. 1939
Merannio	82018	Coaster	Glasgow	Wm. Gray, West Hartlepool	1881	1033	Maclay & McIntyre, Glasgow	Beached at Tel Aviv, Aug 1939
Rippingham Grange	109983	Steel	London	Belfast	1898	3794	Houlder Line, London	Torpedoed in the Atlantic, May 1917

Name	Reg. No.	Type of Ship	Port of Registry	Where built	Year	Tons	Owner	Notes
Cragoswald	110332	Steel	Newcastle	Port Glasgow	1899	2045	George Lunn, Newcastle	Torpedoed in the Atlantic, April 1917
Loch Etive	78565	Ship	Pointhouse	A & J Inglis, Glasgow	1877	1234	James Lilburn, Glasgow	Sold as a hulk in 1911
Sardinian	71695	Iron	Glasgow	Greenock	1887	2788	Allan Line, Glasgow	Sold as coal hulk at Vigo, 1920
Kensington Star		Steamship		Glasgow	1893	8669	Red Star Line	Scrapped 1910
Deania		Iron			1866			
Fernside	87355	Iron	Glasgow	Sunderland	1898	1226	John Gaff, Glasgow	
Leila	86637	Iron	London	Whitby	1882	925	Maclay & Macintyre, Glasgow	Sunk by a mine, in the North Sea Dec. 1939

List of Illustrations

Glossary

Barque – a three-masted vessel with the fore-mast square-rigged, and the main-mast and mizzen-mast fore-and-aft rigged.

Belay – to fasten a running rope by coiling it round a cleat or belaying-pin.

Brigantine (Brig) – a two-masted square-rigged vessel.

Clew up – to truss or tie up sails to the yards.

Coaster – a vessel engaged in coastal trade.

Davit – one of a pair of pieces of timber or iron, projecting over the ship's side or stern, having tackle to raise a boat by.

Deep-water ships – large sailing ships.

Derrick – an apparatus for lifting weights, closely resembling a crane.

Donkey-engine – a small engine used in steam vessels for loading and unloading, pumping water into the boilers.

Falls – lowering or hoisting ropes

Fife-rail – the rail round the main mast for belaying-pins.

Forecastle, fo'c'sle – a short raised deck at the fore-end of a vessel: the forepart of the ship under the maindeck, the quarters of the crew.

Gasket – a canvas band used to bind the sails to the yards when furled.

Gin – machine for hoisting

Greenhorn – a raw, inexperienced youth.

Mizzen-mast – in a three-masted vessel the mast nearest the stern.

Royal mast – the fourth and highest part of the mast

Schooner – swift sailing vessel, generally two-masted, rigged either with fore-and-aft sails on both masts or with square top and topgallant sails on the foremast.

Tackle – the ropes, rigging etc of a ship.

Yard – a long beam on a mast for spreading square sails.

Yard-arm – either half of a ship's yard (right or left) from the centre to the end.